Hot Jobs & Amazing Careers
Smart Moves for Paralegals

Chere B. Estrin

Also Available From Estrin LegalEd

The Big Book of Vendors
Organizing Your Attorney
The Quick Guide to Summarizing Depositions

Other Books by Chere Estrin

The Paralegal Career Guide Third Edition (PrenticeHall)
The Successful Paralegal's Job Search Guide
(ThomsonDelmar)

Career Columns by Chere Estrin

Legal Assistant Today magazine (James Publishing)

Hot Jobs & Amazing Careers
Smart Moves for Paralegals

Chere B. Estrin

Estrin LegalEd
Los Angeles, CA

ISBN 978-1-60402-692-4

This publication is designed to provide accurate and authoritative information in regard to the subject matter covered. It is sold with the understanding that neither the author nor the publisher is engaged n rendering legal, accounting, or other professional services. If legal advice or other expert assistance is required, the services of a competent professional person should be sought.

-From a Declaration of Principles jointly adopted by a Committee of the American Bar Association and a Committee of Publishers.

Estrin LegalEd books are available at special quantity discounts to use as premiums and sales promotions, or for use in corporate training programs. For more information, please write to the Director of Special Sales, Professional Publishing, Estrin LegalEd, 11271 Ventura Blvd., Studio City, CA 91604. You may e-mail us at info@EstrinLegalEd.com or contact your local bookstore.

To Dana Brody and Hilary Brody
Thank Heaven for my girls

Note to Readers:

The job descriptions in this book have been designed to indicate the general nature and level of work performed by paralegals. It is not designed to contain or be interpreted as a comprehensive inventory of all duties, responsibilities, and qualifications required of any employees.

Positions in this book are compilations of several positions or represent past positions unless otherwise indicated. If an employer is listed, it does not mean the position is available now. Positions are listed to encourage you to conduct the appropriate research and seek out similar jobs.

Table of Contents

Preface

Preface

Until I began the research for this book, I thought I pretty much knew all there was to know about the paralegal field. With over 20 years in paralegal management, staffing and education, I was pretty certain that I had witnessed just about every possible position. How wrong I was!

While I was aware that the field was moving and expanding rapidly, I was unaware that it had extended to just about every walk of industry and practice specialty. As I got further and further into digging up paralegal job descriptions, careers, employers, positions, and more, I learned that there were no limits as to what companies, government agencies or law firms might be hiring.

Because of the enormous job possibilities for paralegals, I have stayed within the legal field. Alternative positions utilizing your paralegal background outside of law is a subject for another book entirely. If you are enjoying yourself in this field but want to be aware of what is going on in your field, this book is for you. You don't even have to be searching for another position to glean how you might expand your own position right where you are now.

I have researched thousands of paralegal positions and selected just some of those for representation purposes here. Frankly, this book could have been three or four times the size it is now. Many of the job descriptions are a compilation of several want ads or postings for paralegals unless otherwise specified. For those job descriptions that mention an employer, please bear in mind that these descriptions are representative of the type of position and qualifications the employer may have been seeking at one point. It does not represent any open positions at this point. The point is to raise your awareness as to who hires paralegals and give you an idea about hiring requirements.

The purpose of this book is to give you just a sampling of what law firms, government agencies, vendors and companies hire paralegals and the skills, experience and education generally required. Because the organization may be represented by one or two types of paralegal positions, does not mean that there aren't others. The company may not be hiring right now but you never know what might happen in the near future. Check with these organizations to see what openings are currently available and find out whether the qualifications required for those positions have changed.

It is important that you use this book to launch your research into your job search or expansion of your career and not as a final authority because of the speed in which things change. Use your attention to detail, factual investigation and organizational skills to do a thorough search to find just the right position. I have given you types of positions, areas of law, sampling of law firms, corporate legal departments, vendors and government agencies that have hired or are interested in hiring paralegals. Use these as a foundation.

Writing your resume, cover letter and performing the necessary follow-up can be found in another book that I've written, *The Successful Paralegal's Job Search Guide* (ThomsonDelmar). That book has 50 sample resumes and over 250 questions you can be asked on the interview. As of this writing, you can get it at www.amazon.com or www.barnesandnoble.com or ask for it at your local bookstore.

If you think you are stuck in your career, you are not. If you think that as an entry-paralegal you might not find the right job, look again. The field is flexible in its requirements, open to your background and full of unexpected surprises in who hires paralegals. The only thing that is limiting you is you.

Rather than a jungle, I can only say, it's a Candyland out there. Here's to outrageous success and the best of luck in your new adventure!

Chere B. Estrin
Los Angeles, CA
July, 2007

Chapter One

Choices, Choices and More Choices
The Hottest Jobs Today

Whether you are an entry-level paralegal or a seasoned pro, at some point in your career you're going to stop and take time out to look around and find out what job options are available to you. It doesn't matter if you're already working in a law firm, in-house legal department of a corporation, government agency, for a vendor, non-profit organization or the military. The reality is you are not stuck, despite your best persuasive arguments with yourself. Career options today for paralegals at all levels are more than you have probably ever realized.

Because the most common paralegal jobs are usually in law firms, paralegals often overlook new and exciting careers outside of the a litigation paralegal position, the most common denominator. Did you know that you could become a paralegal for the Getty Museum? How about the CIA? Can you imagine yourself working in the corporate world on money-laundering issues for JPMorganChase? Perhaps you'd like to go into the corporate world and work for Weight Watchers. You may picture yourself working for a government agency on tough environmental issues and join the hot global warming controversy. Ever picture yourself in an entertainment position working with top film stars? How about a non-profit organization such as the

Make-A-Wish Foundation or joining the military and traveling around the world?

These and other exciting paralegal positions are available all over the country and beyond. Gone are the days when the paralegal position was simply a minor evolution of the legal secretarial position. The paralegal has taken over many of the duties of associates and there seems to be no limit of the sophisticated level of assignments a paralegal can handle – without the actual practicing of law, of course. However, the demographics have changed little. It's still a pink collar field. In 2005, only 13.5% of paralegals were men.

Paralegals are found in all types of organizations, but most are employed by law firms, corporate legal departments, and various government offices. In these organizations, they can work in many different areas of the law, including litigation, personal injury, corporate law, criminal law, employee benefits, intellectual property, labor law, bankruptcy, immigration, family law, and real estate. As the law has become more complex, paralegals have responded by becoming more specialized. Within specialties, functions often are broken down further so that paralegals may deal with a specific area. For example, paralegals specializing in labor law may concentrate exclusively on employee benefits.

The Labor Department

The Labor Department states that paralegals and legal assistants held about 224,000 jobs in 2004. This figure seems low. The number is most likely higher because while many job descriptions fit those of a paralegal, the position may carry a different title such as legal analyst, litigation support staff, trial specialist, assistant corporate secretary, legal assistant, collections analyst and more.

Private law firms employ 7 out of 10 paralegals and legal assistants; most of the remainder work for corporate legal departments and various levels of government. Within the Federal Government, the U.S. Department of Justice is the largest employer, followed by the Social Security Administration and the U.S. Department of the Treasury. A small number of paralegals own their own businesses. They work as freelance legal assistants, contracting their services to attorneys or corporate legal departments. Many work as temps.

Most paralegals have an associate's degree in paralegal studies, or a bachelor's degree coupled with a certificate in paralegal studies.

The Department of Labor once classified the paralegal field as one of the fastest growing fields. While that statement is no longer true, employment is projected to grow much faster than average through 2014 as employers try to reduce costs by hiring paralegals to perform tasks formerly carried out by lawyers. The DOL's research shows that competition for jobs should continue and experienced, formally trained paralegals should have the best employment opportunities.

The DOL further predicts demand for paralegals is expected to grow as an expanding population increasingly requires legal services, particular in areas such as intellectual property, health care, international law, elder issues, criminal law, and environmental law. Federal, State, and local government agencies, consumer organizations, and the courts also should continue to hire paralegals in increasing numbers. Paralegals specializing in areas such as real estate, bankruptcy, medical malpractice, and product liability should have ample opportunities.

The growth of prepaid legal plans also should contribute to the demand for legal services. Paralegal employment is expected to increase as organizations presently employing paralegals assign them a growing range of tasks and as paralegals are increasingly employed in small and medium-size establishments. A growing number of experienced paralegals are expected to establish their own businesses such as litigation support, e-discovery/forensics, trial graphics, compliance, corporate filings and other related services.

Current Salaries for Entry-Level and Experienced Paralegals

Salaries for paralegals are all over the board. Further in this book, we'll show you the latest survey data from *Legal Assistant Today* (LAT) magazine. Salaries for paralegals are based on market-rate, demand, years in the field, education, geographic location, size of employer, experience and practice specialty.

In its latest report, the DOL stated that paralegals working for large law firms or in large metropolitan areas earn more than those working for smaller firms or in less populated regions. In addition to earning a salary, many paralegals receive bonuses. In May 2004, full-time wage and salary paralegals and legal assistants had median annual earnings, including bonuses, of $39,130. The middle 50 percent earned between $31,040 and $49,950. The top 10 percent earned more than $61,390. The bottom 10 percent earned less than $25,360.

The International Paralegal Management Association (IPMA) has very different figures. This may be based upon the fact that most of the respondents to their survey hail from major firms or Fortune 500 in-house legal departments. IPMA's survey for 2006 shows Paralegal Managers earned an average of $102,000 and senior paralegals averaging slightly above $70,000.

According to www.LawCrossing.com, the annual salary of a paralegal can range anywhere from $24,000 to more than $61,000. The median salary of a paralegal is roughly $33,000. Another 2007 survey from PayScale, Inc. indicates that the median salary of a paralegal in Los Angeles is $48,000, clearly demonstrating where you are located and size of city does matter.

Some firms give higher salaries and more benefits to paralegals with specific qualifications. Educational level is an important factor. Paralegals who have bachelor's degrees or go through certification programs will usually command higher salaries than those who do not as will paralegals with more experience and who demonstrate the ability to execute sophisticated assignments.

There is potential to do very well financially as a paralegal. Patsy Carr, the director the paralegal program at George Washington University in Washington, D.C., voiced an encouraging trend, stating that third-year paralegals were earning, on average, $38,000. This reflects a substantial increase from paralegals' average entry-level salaries in the low to mid-20s.

Paralegals usually start at a minimum of around $25,000 per year ($35-40,000 in Los Angeles) and, as can work their way to upwards of $60,000 per year or more depending upon the city you are located. Benefits tend to be excellent, including paid health/dental insurance, two to four weeks of vacation, sick leave, substantial bonuses, and 401(k) plans. Benefits in corporate law departments look to be even better than those in law firms.

Let's explore the career by first examining the hottest positions in the country. After that, we'll move to positions you may never even have thought of or known existed for paralegals.

The Hottest Jobs in America for Paralegals

A "hot" job is defined by the position's value in the market place. In order to be a "hot" job, there must be:

1.   A high demand by employers;

2.   A lack of plentiful, qualified candidates;

3.   A difficult time filling open positions;

4.   A pay-scale that is higher than usual.

Also qualifying as a "hot" job are those positions that are in constant demand by employers with an unending need, such as litigation. No matter what tone the economy has set, litigation will always be present.

This list changes according to the market and economic conditions. The most important thing to remember is what is hot today may be colder than Alaska in the winter tomorrow. What is hot in your region may be laughable in another. For example, Trusts & Estates may be booming in the Sun Belt area where boomers go to retire but nowhere near as hot in Wisconsin. By "hottest" we are referring to those positions with the most demand, not necessarily the highest paying.

The Hot List

(Not necessarily in order of popularity)

1. Business litigation

2. Intellectual Property

3. Compliance – Corporate Governance

4. Corporate Securities

5. Corporate Maintenance in large corporate legal departments

6. Civil litigation

7. Contract Specialists

8. Mergers & Acquisitions

9. Litigation Support & e-Discovery

10. Trial Specialists

Add to this list positions within a corporate legal setting in many different practice specialties and you'll have a pretty complete list. Bear in mind, the "hot" list changes as the economy changes. A recession brings a need for bankruptcy paralegals; a hot stock market brings a need for mergers & acquisition specialists and real estate paralegals. A downturn in the economy and those same paralegals are beating the pavement in search of a new position.

A Look at Specialties

1. Business litigation

While others in the field may not consider business litigation as one of the hottest specialties, we decided it belongs on the list because of its never-ending demand. Few law firms of any size do not handle some sort of business litigation. In this era of fast-track trials, do-it-yourself-law, influence from TV lawyer shows and more, litigation does not appear that it's going to go away any time soon. Scan any of the want ads, job sites or law firm websites, and you'll see thousands of jobs for litigation paralegals.

2. Intellectual Property

The Internet ushered in a new era for hot specialties for paralegals. Trademarks, copyrights and patents have exploded in numbers. Unfortunately, there are few, if any, paralegal certificates awarded in the area of Intellectual Property. Training is usually received on-the-job and few lawyers have time to train. The demand for skilled paralegals in IP has increased significantly over the past 5-7 years. It is a highly-paid position found almost anywhere in the country.

3. Compliance – Corporate Governance

Unless you've been on a desert island for the past 7 years and totally isolated from any kind of business news, you must have heard about the Sarbanes-Oxley Act. With the fall of Enron, Congress decided it was time to make public corporations accountable for its actions. Combine SOX with the increased trend in expansion of corporate legal departments and hundreds of new paralegal positions were born.

4. Corporate Securities

Working with the SEC, handling securities transactions for law firms or corporate legal departments or even working for the SEC itself has become big business. Lawyers have either relented or are relieved to hand over more sophisticated assignments to paralegals and that action in itself has led to an increase in hard-to-find corporate paralegals who are knowledgeable in the area of securities.

5. Corporate Maintenance

Law firms handle business clients who have no interest or knowledge in updating corporate minute books, issuing notices to shareholders, or any other duties the upkeep of the documents a corporation would require to keep current. You might be involved in the formation of a corporation, LLC or other entities. You might even work for a large corporation and handle all of its subsidiaries.

You could work in a law firm handling hundreds of small clients such as dentists or doctors; you could handle a few large corporate clients such as Fortune 500 corporations or you might work directly for the client itself. Huge Fortune 500 corporations might have as many as 400 subsidiaries that must be maintained. The need for corporate structure formation and maintenance now extends to foreign clients and there doesn't seem to be an end in sight.

6. Civil Litigation

Civil litigation addresses a myriad of cases from personal injury to environmental; real estate to intellectual property, toxic tort, lemon law, insurance, family law – in other words, anything that is not criminal. There is always a demand for civil litigation paralegals. While this area does not meet the "hot list" criteria of paying more than the normal for the position, civil litigation does not "go away". If you want to be assured of finding a position just about anywhere in the country, you will find it in civil litigation.

7. Contracts

A contracts paralegal handles drafting of purchase agreements, form contracts, contracts used by the client or corporation, boiler plate forms, and more. Contracts paralegals are not that easy to find. In an ever increasing litigious society, companies want to make sure that they are covered in any situation. Here is another situation where lawyers have turned over previously thought-of associate duties to savvy paralegals.

8.   Mergers & Acquisitions

It's a dog-eat-dog world - one company gobbling up another. Of course, the highs and lows of M&A depend on a thriving or downturn economy. A paralegal specializing in M&A would need to understand closing documents, legal documents pertaining to the merger; and be able to withstand long hours and anxious clients.

9.   Litigation Support and e-Discovery

There probably isn't a more booming area than litigation support and e-Discovery. Nor is there a more perfect area for a paralegal to advance. The new Rules of Federal Discovery passed late 2006 ushered in a new era in discovery along with new terminology. It's a highly paid area with all too many people learning on the job. At this writing, other than a couple of entry courses in a paralegal program, there is no where you can go to get a degree or certificate in litigation support. The area continues to boom.

10.   Trial Specialists

As with lawyers, few paralegals actually get to go to trial. Those that do face an impossible task: learn on the job or be eaten alive! Knowing how to set up a War Room; set up the courtroom; handle exhibits, witnesses and bailiffs; prepare summaries of daily transcripts are only a small part of what a trial specialist does. While this is not a position that is widely advertised, employers are willing to pay more dollars for those with heavy trial experience. Here is another situation of attorneys turning over previously thought of associate duties to competent paralegals.

Michael Satz

Civil Litigation Paralegal
Small Firm, Florida

The Sunshine State Paralegal

If you would like to meet a paralegal who has found "the good life", Michael Satz is probably the one. As probably one of the few paralegals to receive a car as part of his perks, Satz, an athletic, high-energy, fun-loving man in his forties, talks frankly about his 14-year paralegal career, education and benefits of working in the Sunshine State of Florida.

Tell us about the law firm and the practice specialties of your firm.
I work in a small practice with less than 10 attorneys. We practice in the areas of Civil Litigation, family law, small claims court, and administrative law.

What is your background including your paralegal education?
I have a B.S. in Paralegal Studies from Kaplan University (Summa Cum Laude) that I obtained on-line, and an A.S. in Paralegal Studies that I earned from Florida Metropolitan University. At FMU, I graduated Magna Cum Laude. I was also the Past President of Kappa Lambda, the Paralegal Honor Society of Kaplan University. I am also a certificated Master Legal Researcher by Westlaw, and was granted the honor of being a *Paralegal Superstar* by Paralegalgateway.com (Paralegal Gateway).

Did the fact that you held a certificate from an online paralegal school make it difficult or easy for you to find a position? Or, was it a non-issue?
Very easy, in fact, I was quite amazed at how easy it was to obtain my first paralegal position. Qualified paralegals are in high demand in the South Florida area, and the ones with a BS are highly sought after in this market.

What was the reaction from employers regarding your online certificate?
It was a non-event. When they asked where I earned my degree, I advised I earned it from FMU or Kaplan; indeed, it was never raised as an issue that I earned my degrees on-line. After being promoted, I really found out that no one cares as long as you can do the work required.

Tell us about your assignments and a little bit about your day.
That is a difficult task to state, as each day is *completely* different. I often attend and argue cases at mediation for our clients in small claims court and in administrative law courts. I also assist in trial preparation for our circuit and appellate court cases. I prepare pleadings, investigate defendants, contact opposing counsel, assist in the negotiation of cases, research cases and statutes online, and perform a plethora of other duties. I am also the computer network administrator for our office computer systems, as I have a high degree of computer knowledge.

I'm sure it hasn't always been easy. Where have you found toughest challenges?
Raising a precocious son as a "single guy," i.e. it is great to know the law, but getting a wayward teenage son to make his bed is quite a challenge.

What has been the most fun or the greatest reward for you?
When we won a big case, part of the settlement for attorney fees was a number of vacations to Jamaica to our firm. The Senior Partner gave me one of them; an all expenses paid, all-inclusive trip to Negril, Jamaica.

What are salaries like in a small firm? Are they good, bad or right in there?
Excellent. Typically, Senior Civil Litigation paralegals earn in the top tier of paralegals in the South Florida region.

What is the best method or technique for finding jobs? Or more specifically, do you have any secrets you'd like to share about job-searching?
I cheated. I used spam to get the attention of potential employers. Due to my computer knowledge, I combined my IT knowledge of computers with my research on local attorneys to become employed in less than two weeks.

Here are the steps I took:

    a. I created a database of all the local attorneys that I MIGHT be interested in interviewing for a potential job. I looked in the Yellow pages for ONLY attorneys in my immediate zip code.

b. I looked up each one and entered the attorney's email addresses right off the Florida bar Web site.

c. This gave me the actual e-mail address for each potential employer and the attorney's address, and company affiliation and the areas of practice.

d. After loading this information into my database, I created a mail merge for a cover letter and e-mail template of my resume.

e. This allowed me to e-mail hundreds of potential employers my resume and cover letter introducing my background and me.

f. After my first barrage of emails, I followed up each one with a phone call to the prospective employer and deleted all those non-interested attorneys.

g. Next, I sent another barrage of emails (SPAM works!) and followed up with additional phone calls two days later. The phone calls also told me who might be "potentially interested."

h. Thereafter, I sent a third batch of e-mails and made my third set of phone calls. Each time I winnowed down the list substantially to a working number of "real potentials." I then scheduled the interviews accordingly.

i. I was interviewed by over ten firms, hired by three, and created a bidding war on benefits, salary and bonuses.

j. Ultimately, I chose one firm that matched my "style," and have become the Senior Partner's "right hand man." In just the second year of my employment with the firm, they signed off on a Chrysler Sebring Convertible as a bonus and hopefully, I will retire here.

k. I never looked in the want ads, I never networked using the normal tools, and I was employed in less than two weeks after I started my e-mail campaign.

Tell us what aspect of your job do you enjoy the most?
The diversity. Every single day is different and I never know what the next day's challenge will be or where my job will take me.

You make this sound like it is all just a lot of fun. What do you like least?
The hours. We have long hours here and often, our family lives' suffer. In litigation, often we prepare for a hearing or trial throughout the weekend, and 70-hour weeks are not unheard of in this office.

What advice would you give other paralegals seeking to get into your specialty?
STUDY: Make yourself a prime "go to person." In other words, know the case files, the documents, the evidence, the case law; stop thinking like a secretary, a file clerk or a receptionist, and think of yourself as THE person actually arguing the case. How would you win? What evidence proves your client's case? What witnesses will testify to what matters?

Moreover, know the local rules of your court and read the law pertaining to that area of law. Lots of attorneys "believe" they know the law, but as it changes often, they really have outdated information. It is our job to know the latest information and to advise the case attorney accordingly. Thus, we must know how to find the law, to Shepardize it accordingly and assist to win the cases for our clients.

Did you start out in another specialty?
Yes, I started in family law, but I love civil litigation.

Even though you work long hours, you seem like a person who probably has a life outside of the firm. What do you do for fun?
I fly airplanes (I am a student pilot getting ready to take my license exam), canoe, kayak, camp, scuba dive (I am a Master Scuba diver), rock climb, water ski, and a host of other activities. I am an adventure junky and anything on land, air or sea, I will try. Best of all, I live in South Florida; notwithstanding the occasional hurricane, we have awesome weather all year long.

Busy schedule! Do you seek out any professional activities?
I have a love for law and go to all of the continuing legal education courses I can. I am also active in a number of paralegal related activities and legal listservs on the Internet.

Are you looking forward to the future? If so, what is your next step?
I am working on my law license on-line through Concord Law School; the first online law school in the country.

How would you like to give us some words of wisdom?
Moneymaking: To earn top monies, you have to bring in money as well. This means, when you are dealing with your clients and have, for example, settled a case, advise the client your firm also handles, real estate, closings, wills, trusts, estates, whatever. Make sure the client has an email address so they can email you…make it personal so they want to come back to the firm.

Offer to take on ANY job in the law firm so that you can interact more with the clients. This will invariably mean the client will call you and you can schedule the interview. When the interview occurs, be in the office with the attorney. The firm will know you handled the matter to get the client in, and thus, you will be more valuable to the firm.

Additionally, be the person who knows the most about a given case. When someone has a question, invariably, the partner, associate, manager, etc. will come to you for the answers. If you have the answers, you become more valuable.

Finally, do the job. This means, if you have to run to the Courthouse for a filing deadline…do it. Our jobs are precious, and if it is not valuable to you then leave. Do not be caught at a company you do not want to work for; if the job is not exactly what you want, find another. If the senior partner tells me we need copies and the copier is broken, I will try to fix it. If the slide show of evidence is not perfect for our trial, I will work on it until it is "just right." We have to be the ones to accept ownership of a case and thus, ensure we provide all we can to zealously advocate on behalf of our clients. In my mind, the "bottom line" is you have to love the job and be willing to do whatever is required to assist the attorneys in the case.

Hot Tip

Don't be shy about joining your local paralegal association. Not enough can be said about the benefits of networking, dismissed by so many.

Look at it this way: who is the first person you confide in when you are thinking about leaving your job? Human Resources? Hardly.

It's your colleagues. They know when there's going to be a position in their firm long before supervisors. Get next to them at a paralegal meeting.

They have valuable information you need!

Chapter Two

Today's Educated Paralegal
What You Need to Succeed

Today, there is an estimated 1,000 colleges and universities, law schools, and proprietary schools offer formal paralegal training programs. Approximately 260 paralegal programs are approved by the American Bar Association (ABA). Although many programs do not require such approval, graduation from an ABA-approved program can enhance your employment opportunities. The requirements for admission to these programs vary. Some require certain college courses or a bachelor's degree; others accept high school graduates or those with legal experience. There are a few schools giving a standardized test including the GMAT or other tests and personal interviews

Paralegal programs include 2-year associate degree's programs, 4-year bachelor's degree programs, and certificate programs that can take only a few months to complete. Most certificate programs provide intensive and, in some cases, specialized paralegal training for individuals who already hold college degrees, while associate's and bachelor's degree programs usually combine paralegal training with courses in other academic subjects.

The latest entry into paralegal training is the online school. These schools have popped up to meet an ever-increasing need in paralegal education. While not widely accepted as yet by many employers, many online schools are run by very credible attorneys and educators seeking to meet today's needs. As of this writing, no online school has been ABA approved.

The quality of paralegal training programs varies; the better programs usually include job placement services. Programs generally offer courses introducing students to the legal applications of computers, including how to perform legal research on the Internet. Many paralegal training programs also offer an internship in which students gain practical experience by working for several months in a private law firm, the office of a public defender or attorney general, a bank, a corporate legal department, a legal aid organization, or a government agency. Don't overlook the value of an internship when seeking a job after graduation. Check with recent graduates about their job seeking experiences before enrolling in any paralegal program.

Although most employers do not require certification, earning a voluntary certificate from a professional association may offer advantages. The National Association of Legal Assistants (NALA), for example, has established standards for certification requiring various combinations of education and experience. Paralegals who meet these standards are eligible to take a 2-day examination, given three times each year at several regional testing centers. Those who pass this examination may use the Certified Legal Assistant (CLA) designation.

NALA also offers an advanced paralegal certification for those who want to specialize in other areas of the law. In addition, the Paralegal Advanced Competency Exam, administered through the National Federation of Paralegal Associations, offers professional recognition to paralegals with a bachelor's degree and at least 2 years of experience. Those who pass this examination may use the Registered Paralegal (RP) designation.

Toni Marsh, Esq.
Assistant Professor and Director
George Washington University
Paralegal Studies Program
Washington, D.C.

Straight Talk from a Top Paralegal Educator

GW University Offers Masters Program for Paralegals

Toni Marsh, Esquire has been the Assistant Professor and Director of the George Washington University paralegal studies master's degree and graduate certificate programs. Her outgoing personality has helped strengthen this already well-known and well-respected paralegal program for two years.

Tell us a little about your background. I understand you have quite a history in paralegal education at various universities. Presently, I am the assistant professor at the George Washington University and the director of the GW paralegal studies master's degree and graduate certificate programs. Prior to coming to GW, I was the director of the paralegal studies program at University of North Carolina. I have fifteen years teaching experience at The George Washington University, Georgetown University, and Cuyahoga Community College.

What do you do as the Assistant Profession and Director of the program?
I designed and developed the GW program and the UNC program. I also teach American jurisprudence, legal writing, and juvenile law and am the author of *Juvenile Law* and *American Jurisprudence for Paralegals*.

What was your background before GW? Did you practice law?
I was a practicing juvenile and criminal defense attorney for 17 years before I decided to enter the world of paralegal education. Right now, I am also a volunteer at the DC Superior Court's Family Law Self Help Center.

Tell us more about the GW paralegal program.
The George Washington University College of Professional Studies, in association with the GW Law School, offers a 32-credit master's degree in paralegal studies, one of the few paralegal studies master's degrees in the country, and an 18-credit graduate certificate in paralegal studies.

In order to take full advantage of our location in the Nation's capital and our affiliation with one of the finest law schools in the country, we offer legal specialties in government law, intellectual property law, and international law.

GW law librarians teach legal research and students have access to the GW law library. Paralegal students are invited to GW Law School functions. GW Law School Dean Frederick M. Lawrence and Jacob Burns Law Library Director Scott M. Pagel serve on the Paralegal Studies Program Advisory Board.

Each course includes an integration of instruction in ethics, professionalism, and legal technology. This interweaving of content into the curriculum ensures that students will internalize these concepts and master these skills naturally.

The program combines classroom-based and online instruction delivered via Blackboard, GW's Internet-based course delivery platform. This allows instructors to supplement their materials with links to original documents, narrated power point lectures that expand upon concepts introduced in class, audio, video, and other multimedia instructional materials. Students participate in online discussions, self-assessments, and group activities.

The program encourages, promotes, and facilitates student participation in pro bono programs, which provides students the opportunity to gain real world experience and form valuable relationships in the legal community while serving the community. Pro bono activity instills community service awareness in students at a time when they are forming their legal philosophy and ethos.

Where are the hot jobs in Washington DC and around the country?
The hottest jobs right now are in intellectual property, international law and trade, government contracts, litigation, and immigration.

There is a trend in Washington DC to hire paralegals to fill positions previously occupied by attorneys. Law firms, government agencies, and the international banks are all doing it.

Tell us about these interesting positions within the government.
Just yesterday I received a phone call from a senior attorney for one of the highest offices in the government. They currently have a small group of paralegals and are seeking to expand that group and have these paralegals perform some of the tasks attorneys had previously managed. The paralegals they hire will conduct extensive research, draft documents, work closely with primary government documents, and have contact with some very high-ranking clients.

In addition to the exciting work, the benefits and working conditions in the federal government are excellent.

What do employers look for in entry-level and experienced level paralegals?
Good research and writing skills and mastery of technology are crucial.

What are the most important skills a paralegal can offer an employer?
Poise, professionalism; attention to detail; commitment to the organization's vision and mission; strong, clear, accurate writing; technological adroitness; comprehensive and dogged research skills; determination; self-motivation

What message do you have about continuing legal education for paralegals?
Continuing education is essential for all paralegals. The law is constantly changing, as are the tools and techniques paralegals must master. The legal profession is one of the most demanding of professional currency and competence – and the most unforgiving of a lack thereof.

How do you think paralegals can advance their careers?
Stay current in their fields; continue their education; become involved in professional associations; attend conferences, seminars, workshops, and lectures; read the literature professional literature

What's the most important advice you can give paralegals today?
Love what you do, work hard, never stop learning.

Hot Tip

View your career much like a chess game. Think ahead, plan your moves and strategize. That way, you will be less of a victim to circumstance and more in control of your own destiny.

Chapter Three

Where to Look for the
Perfect Paralegal Position

When you think of where you'd like to work, the first thing you want to consider is, frankly, what do you like? If you are a pet lover, perhaps you want to land with an attorney that specializes in animal rights. If you envision yourself in the corporate world, consider any one of the thousands of corporate legal department positions. A corporation that is as small as $20 million in sales may hire a general counsel who in turn, hires a paralegal. You don't have to work for a huge corporation in order to enter the corporate legal department.

Have a desire to work with the public? Get out your investigative skills and research immigration, family law or pro bono work. The City Attorney's office in your community probably utilizes paralegals to work with the public. You may find yourself working in the court system or even a corporation that does community outreach. Community outreach could include informative sessions given to the public; working with inner-cities, setting up trusts or more.

The key to finding the right job is to remember that you are only as effective as the research you do. Skimming the local paper and perusing Monster.com occasionally will get you corresponding minimal results. Here's a guarantee – the job will not automatically come to you. You can wish, you can dream, you can whine, you can complain. Unless you conduct extensive, *ongoing* research, exert hard work, discipline and dedication to the search, you will stay in your current scenario. It's that simple.

Types of Organizations Hiring Paralegals

Here are the structures of organizations that hire paralegals:

1. Law firms
   a. Solo practitioners
   b. Small firms
   c. Mid-Sized firms
   d. Large firms
   e. Mega firms (over 1,000 attorneys)

2. Corporate Legal Departments (law departments within a corporation)

3. The Government
   a. Federal
   b. State
   c. City
   d. Agencies

4. Non-profit organizations

5. Temporary help/staffing organizations

6. Vendors to the legal community

7. The Military

8. Private schools and universities

9. The virtual world

April Piercey, CLA, Corporate Paralegal
Corporate Legal Department

In-House to In-House
It's A Good Life

A vivacious 40-something paralegal, April Piercey recently took a position with a start-up company in Silicon Valley, California. A solid background in real estate, credit finance and mortgage banking, made her a sure-fit for this entrepreneurial hi-tech company with an exciting future.

"I have a variety of interesting assignments, kind of a "do-everything" position," she says. "I am involved in corporate compliance, contracts, shareholder compliance, HR, insurance implementation, and all aspects of managing a start-up company. It's exciting and I'm having a great time".

Piercey has over 12 years as a paralegal. She transferred from a former career in real estate, credit finance and mortgage banking leveraging her real estate financing experience to become a paralegal.

A proponent of the CLA designation given through the National Association for Legal Assistants (NALA), Piercey says here greatest career challenge was the three solid months of studying for the CLA exam. At the same time, her greatest reward was, "Receiving my CLA designation and giving back to the paralegal community through my involvement with the Paralegal Association of Santa Clara County (California) and local educational opportunities.

Finding her current position through a friend, she realizes that her salary is within the limitations of a start-up company. However, she knows that the hard work is bound to pay off and the entrepreneurial spirit of the company is refreshing and motivating. She feels like she's able to reach new career heights.

"My background as a real estate and corporate paralegal for so many years plus my former career paid off," she says. "I was the Loan Servicing Manager for a company with a large portfolio of Freddie Mac, Fannie Mae and Government loans".

Piercey believes paralegals gain great benefits by participating in their local paralegal associations. As President of the Paralegal Association of Santa Clara County ("PASCCO"), she has had an opportunity to get involved in successful efforts to promote the paralegal field. As an instructor, Estrin LegalEd and instructor in Paralegal Studies at West Valley College, she has found a great deal of joy watching as paralegals learn and absorb new techniques and procedures. Add to her credit authoring *The Paralegal's Role in Construction Loans"* and you have a paralegal right at the top of her career.

Hot Tip:

Be sure to research overtime issues in any new position. Many positions, particularly litigation jobs in law firms demand many overtime hours. Be sure to calculate travel time as well.

Chapter Four
Choosing New Practice Specialties

Paralegals are in every law practice specialty available. You may decide that you enjoy a certain area of law and the type of industry is not particularly important to you. On the other hand, you may have a fantasy of working with particular people, level of education, or industry that is important to you. Your task ahead is to find law firms, corporations, government agencies that specialize in the type of law that appeals to you.

Aligning the kind of work you want with location is important. If you can't or don't want to move to another city or state to find your dream job, you're going to have to adjust your expectations according to the region's industries. Entertainment law is a strong draw but for those living in a rural area, finding an entertainment law firm may be next to impossible. If, however, you were interested in Indian Law, family law, civil litigation, probate, products liability, personal injury or criminal law, you might be in just the right place.

Areas of Specialties

Here are some general classifications:

Law Classifications

Administrative Law
Appellate Law
Bankruptcy/Debtor/Creditor
Business and Corporation
Civil Rights
Class Actions
Commercial/Consumer Law
Constitutional Law
Criminal Law
Elder Law
Entertainment
Environmental
Ethics
Family

Health Law
Indian Law
Intellectual Property
Labor Law
Municipal Law
Products Liability
Real Property
Special Education
Taxation Tort
Transportation Law
Wills and Estates

Within specific law classifications are niche specialties. Paralegals are used in every aspect of the law. Take a quick look at all the various types of specialties you might find employment. There are even more possibilities than are listed here.

Specialties Within the Classifications

Custody Disputes
Debtor Relations
Discovery
Discrimination
Disposition
District Attorney
Divorce
Drugs and Narcotics
DUI
Easements
Education Law
Eminent Domain
Employee Representation
Employer Representation
Energy
Environmental Law
Estate Administration
Estate Planning

Maritime Law
Mediation/Arbitration
Medical Malpractice
Mergers & Acquisitions
Military/Veteran's Benefits
Motor Vehicles
Lemon Law
Libel and Slander
Litigation
Municipal Law
Natural Resources
Non-profit corporations
Oil and Gas
Public Benefits
Patent
Paternity
Personal Injury
Pharmaceutical

Estates and Trusts
Ethics
Evidence
Farming
Family Law
Finance
Foreclosures
Franchise/Dealership
General Practice
Government Regulations
Health Care
Health Law
Homeowners Association
Insurance
Juvenile
Labor Law
Landlord/Tenant
Legal Affairs of Sr. Citizens
Legal Affairs of the Poor
Legal Malpractice

Preparation of Wills
Probate of Wills
Product Liability
Property
Property Damage
Protection from Abuse
Public Utility Law
Railroads
Real Property
Religion
Residential
Securities
Skills Training
Social Security
Social Security & SST ADM
Social Security Disability
Space Law
Special Education
Sports and Entertainment Law

Taxation
Telecommunications
Tort
Trademark
Traffic
Transportation Law
Trials
Unemployment Compensation
Union Representation
Utilities
Visitation
Water and Water Rights
Wills and Estates
Worker's Compensation
Zoning

Eldonie Etinoff

Immigration Department Supervisor
Pfizer, New York

Fortune 500 Corporation Paralegal

The past seventeen years have been a whirlwind for Eldonie Etinoff. As the Senior Supervisor Immigration for the giant pharmaceutical company, Pfizer, Etinoff has worked her way up the paralegal corporate ladder.

"Immigration law is so complex that I think it deserves a university dedicated to teaching immigration law," she says. Her interest and excitement has held up even after spending almost her entire paralegal career in the same specialty. "I love it. I'm passionate about the work we do as specialists in the field."

Holding a BBA in Business Administration and an MS in Human Resource Management along with a paralegal certificate, Etinoff has leveraged her education and experience into a top position managing the company's immigration program from end-to-end. "I maintain and develop immigration policies and practices," she says. "That includes developing strategy and solutions for complex immigration issues. I also provide training to HR partners, managers and foreign national employees regarding visa processes and legal compliance. I manage outside counsel's relationship and I'm a gatekeeper with regard to the beginning of any immigration-related process."

It's not an easy specialty to get into, according to Etinoff. To train for the position and to become a good immigration paralegal, Etinoff suggests in addition to practical experience, to keep abreast of immigration laws by attending regular seminars; networking with others in the field to learn and share information. "You need to get both academic and hands-on training," she suggests. "In addition, take some courses in Human Resources Management."

"I also manage all immigration applications and visas within the company and supervise the work of immigration specialists I provide supplementary assistance with international immigration issues for expatriate employees. You need to be on top of the latest changes in laws and procedures," she says. "You can never take enough seminars or do enough reading."

While the salary is very good in her position, Etinoff still has tough challenges. Her toughest challenge? "To get managers and HR reps understand that when you have an immigration issue, you must say, "what else?" Simply put immigration does operate in a vacuum." Etinoff stresses the ability to dig deeper by asking the right questions of the right people.

The fast-paced position does have certain stresses. To relieve the stress and have a life outside of the company, the physically-fit, fun-loving, Etinoff loves to take vacations with her husband and is not shy about loving to dine out. "I also like aerobic dancing, taking a nice walk, and exercising," she says.

There are certain parts of the position that remain her favorites such as training, presentations and acting as an Internal Consultant and providing guidance to management; evaluating the case and setting the strategy. "The least favorite part is there are not enough resources," she says.

The rewards are making a difference in the individual's life. "The immigration process affects people's professional and personal lives," she says. "It is really important to pay attention at all times and not make a mistake."

Professional activities are important to her and the advancement of her career. "I'm a member of the SHRM NYC Recruiting Committee and the American Council for International Personnel," she says. She is also active in church.

Keeping in line with other successful paralegals that are always looking toward the future, Etinoff has a career plan. "I'm looking at various options. I have recently started my own business. The purpose is to provide staffing and immigration support to businesses and law firms. Maybe I'll even go to law school."

Chapter Five

Corporate Legal Departments
No More Billable Hours

One of the biggest changes in the legal field today is the number of corporations that have formed their own law firm within the corporation called corporate legal/law departments or in-house law departments. As little as ten years ago, working in a corporation as an attorney or paralegal was not particularly prestigious and did not necessarily pay top dollar.

All of that changed when corporations decided to save legal fees by hiring in-house counsel instead of paying outside law firms. Today, you're likely to see a combination of in-house legal departments and law firms that represent these corporations.

Employers and Law Firms Representing Corporations

Identifying in-house legal departments by researching corporations is one very good way to get a job within a corporate legal department. You can also research the industry to find out the law firms that represent that particular industry. The American Association for Corporate Counsel has thousands of in-house legal departments as members. Plenty of job search websites such as www.lawcrossing.com, list a separate category for researching corporate legal departments. Almost all of the Fortune 500 & 1000 corporations have in-house legal departments from 1 – over 100 attorneys.

Many of the in-house legal departments are spread out throughout the U.S. The corporate headquarters is not always the only office housing a legal department. Some companies such as Starbucks, Prudential, Bank of America, State Farm and others have several offices across the U.S. The most likely candidates for branch in-house legal offices are insurance companies and banks.

Industries That Hire Paralegals and the Law Firms That Support Them

When you think of spending at least 40 hours a week or more in a work environment, be sure you pay attention to the type of industry of the potential job. Those of you currently existing in a burnout situation might not realize that it's not so much the actual work as it is the industry that is burning you out. Sometimes we are so thankful that we've found a position, that at first, focusing on the practice specialty is not an issue. As time goes by, we tend to blame the environment, people, office manager, your colleagues, or routine and repetition

If you are a person who is anti-smoking, then obviously, going to work for a corporation that owns tobacco companies is against your value system. If you are a vegan, believe in anti-global warming measures, use only natural products, then working for a corporation defending itself from environmental clean-up doesn't make sense. Sometimes it's not as clear cut. You could be a Democrat in a Republican firm. You could value work and lifestyle balance but your firm does not concur with your value system. It might even be an age differential.

What corporate legal departments hire paralegals? The list is endless. Almost any company that is considered a Fortune 1-500 probably has an in-house legal department. Because the corporation is headquartered in one location does mean that is the only location paralegals are hired.

Don't overlook there are many more law firms specializing in the same industries as there are corporate legal departments. The industries do not apply strictly to corporations. Here are just 60 industries you can choose. There are many, many more.

Private Sector Industries Hiring Paralegals

1. Banking and mortgage

2. Oil and gas

3. Investment firms

4. Insurance

   a. Auto

   b. Health

   c. Life

     d.   Workers compensation

     e.   Fire

     f.   Casualty

5. Entertainment companies such as movie studios, radio, TV networks, music, record companies

6. Software companies

7. Real estate developers

8. Hotels, resorts and timeshares

9. Travel industry

10. Healthcare

11. Toy companies

12. Publishing companies

13. Manufacturing companies

14. Retail stores

15. Garment/clothing/shoe companies

16. Transportation such as railroads, airlines, automobile, trucking, freight/shipping

17. Hospitals

18. Pharmaceutical companies

19. Chemical companies

20. Nursing homes

21. Grocery stores

22. Pet industry

23. Food industry including produce, coffee, wine, liquor, meat

24. Restaurants

25. Newspapers

26. Utility companies

27. Credit card companies

28. Schools, school districts, colleges, universities

29. Jewelry manufacturers

30. Sports teams and associations

31. Medical equipment

32. Electrical equipment

33. Computer manufacturers

34. Printing

35. Drug stores

36. Staffing

37. Museums

38. Hospitality

39. Recreation

40. Telecommunications including phone companies, cell phones, etc.

41. Internet

42. Consulting

43. Accounting

44. Forensics

45. Fashion & Garment

46. Defense Industry

47. Biotechnology

48. Steel

49. Rubber & Tire

50. High Tech

51. Non-profit organizations

52. Amusement Parks

53. Shipping

54. Building Hardware

55. Computer

56. e-Commerce

57. Airports

58. Automotive

59. Casinos and Gaming

60. Building/Construction

In-House Legal Departments
Partial List

Airlines

American Airlines

Delta Airlines

Jet Blue

United Airlines

Northwest

Airports

Atlanta

John Wayne

Los Angeles

Automotive

Ford

Harley Davidson

Honda

Mercedes Benz

Nissan

Toyota

Porsche

Banks

Bank of America

Citibank

City National Bank

Wells Fargo

J.P. MorganChase

Sumitomo

Suntrust

Big Box Stores

K-Mart

Target

Energy

Wal-Mart

Camera/Film

Eastman Kodak

Car Rental

Hertz

Chemical

Eastman Chemical

Commercial Finance

GE Commercial Finance

Hartford Financial

Prudential

Computers

Dell Computers

Gateway Computers

Hewlett-Packard

Cosmetics

Estee Lauder

Mary Kay

Revlon

Credit/Financial

American Express

Visa

Drug Stores

Longs

Walgreen's

Electronics

Panasonic

Texas Instruments

Sony

Quaker Oats

Valero Energy

Duke Energy

Entertainment

E! Entertainment

Sony Pictures

Fox

Walt Disney

PBS

Universal Studios

Warner Bros.

Turner Broadcasting

MGM

NBC

CBS

CNN

Wide World of Wrestling

WETA Public Television

Showtime

HBO

Screen Actors Guild

WETA

Finance

T. Rowe Price

Smith Barney

Food & Beverage

Coca-Cola

Sara Lee

Anheuser Busch

H.J. Heinz

Kellogg

Pepsi

Safeco

Greeting Cards

American Greeting Cards

Hallmark

Grocery Stores

Krogers

Ralph's

Safeway

The Great A&P

Smart & Final

Healthcare

Health Partners

Heavy Equipment

Caterpillar

John Deere

Home Improvement

The Home Depot

Lowes

Hospitality

Hilton Hotels

Starwood

Marriott

Hospitals

Cedars Sinai

Little Mary of Torrance

Kaiser Permanente

Sisters of Mercy

Insurance

Prudential

Travelers

Nationwide

Farmers Insurance

Valero

The Hartford

State Farm

Geico

Wachovia

20th Century

Interactive Entertainment

Sony Playstation

Square Enix

Internet

AOL

Earthlink

Google

Yahoo!

YouTube

Jewelry

Timex

Tiffany's

Mortgage Banking

Countrywide

Non-Profit Organization

Father Flanagan's Boys Home

Salvation Army

Make-A-Wish Foundation

Juvenile Diabetes Foundation

YMCA

Oil & Gas

Chevron

Occidental Petroleum

Shell Oil

Texaco

ExxonMobil

Starbucks

Online Retail

Amazon.com

Personal Products

Alticor (Amway)

Pharmaceutical

Eli Lilly

Novartis

Ranbaxy

Sanofi Aventis

Wyeth

Publishing

Conde Nast

The Los Angeles Times

Time Warner

Railroads

Union Pacific

Amtrak

Real Estate Developers

Kaufman & Broad

Westfield

D.R. Horton

Centex

Religious

Archdiocese of Los Angeles

Retail Stores

Sears

J.C. Penny

Neiman Marcus

Restaurants

Burger King

McDonalds

Toy Companies

California Pizza Kitchen

Jack-in-the-Box

Islands

Panda Express

Pandera

Software

Adobe

Microsoft

Sage Software

SAP

Space

NASA

Steel

U.S. Steel

Tobacco

Philip Morris

Reynolds

Mattel

Hasbro

Leapfrog

Technology

Seagate Technology

Schlumberger Technology

Microsoft

Apple

SAP America

Universities

Brown University

Stanford University

California State University

Utilities

Southern California Edison

Dept. of Water & Power

North Carolina Cooperative

Examples of Positions in Corporate Legal Departments

Assistant Manager of Risk Administration and Training

Coordinate training programs for personnel safety and purchasing. Oversee duplication of training manuals and materials; prepare legal department communication; prepare minutes and task lists generated from meetings. Edit, track, index and file board resolutions and minutes of meetings. Maintenance of filing system, expense reports and outside counsel invoices.

Real Estate Paralegal - New Store Development

Research real estate property binders, files and documents in connection with property management and operational matters. Coordinate with outside counsel. Answer calls from the field (e.g. stores, district offices, other departments). Handle day-to-day administration of new store development, property management, leases, contracts, inquiries and operational matters.

What You Need to Succeed: Knowledge, skills and abilities acquired through the completion of a bachelor's degree program or equivalent degree in a field of study related to the job.

Real Estate Paralegal – Retail Stores and Restaurants

Review and abstract real estate contracts, leases and operating documents. Work with land development, construction, retail operations and development. Monitor real estate documents from outside counsel and other consultants. Be the primary contact on issues relating to acquisition and leasing of properties. Handle requests from other departments relating to real estate matters, research and review of relevant legal documents.

Litigation Paralegal – Banking, Discovery and Appellate

Assist Bank, inside and outside attorneys in all aspects of litigation. Research, compile and organize case information and documentation; draft pleadings, discovery, bankruptcy and appellate documents; interview colleagues and possible witnesses; summarize depositions and documents; organize case materials utilizing a variety of personal computer software packages. Analyze monitor and resolve routine litigation at the least possible cost.

Draft pleadings including complaints, answers, motions, declarations, writs, default prove-up papers and judgments; drafts discovery requests and responses to discovery; drafts discovery and motions;. Prepare and respond to subpoenas; analyzes and summarizes depositions and documents; drafts default judgment documents. Prepare writs of attachment and possession. Provide legal research and factual investigation.

Insurance/Regulatory – Insurance Industry Expert

Provide research and assistance to the insurance industry, corporate law (including for-profit and non-profit corporations), and association law. Monitor laws and examine the legal, corporate and insurance requirements of multiple states.

Research, draft, analyze and file legal and regulatory documents, including insurance rules, rates and forms in all states. Researching and analyze individual state legal requirements. Research requirements, analyze regulations and maintain and coordinate the insurance licenses for company agents.

Regulatory Compliance in Publicly Held Companies

Coordinate with Legal, Compliance and Business areas to respond to SEC, NASD. Help develop, write and maintain policies and procedures regarding the regulatory examination and inquiry process, and help write and/or review associated training materials. Assist with communicating these procedures to affected personnel in the Company's compliance and operations departments and various distribution channels. Develop and maintain an issues tracking database for all regulatory findings. Prepare written responses to inquiries.

What You Need to Succeed: Bachelor's Degree and relevant professional experience; experience with SEC and NASD broker-dealer and variable product rules; excellent writing skills and experience drafting policies and procedures.

Litigation Paralegal – Commercial Litigation, Franchise

Oversee, organize, and maintain case files associated with various types of commercial litigation that may include franchise, vicarious liability and bankruptcy. Gather and prepare written responses to third party subpoenas. Act as liaison between outside counsel and company personnel to gather information for pleadings, motions, affidavits and discovery requests. Coordinate scheduling of company witnesses for litigation related appearances, review attorney work-product for conformity with company standards and on-going projects related to risk management, litigation management and routine reporting to clients. Basic computer legal research responsibilities.

What You Need to Succeed: Many corporations require a Bachelor's Degree and a paralegal certificate although there are exceptions. Experience as a litigation paralegal in a law firm is generally welcome. The larger the in-house legal department, the more they seem to ask for experience from major or mid-size law firms or a similar in-house legal department. Excellent written and oral communication skills. Experience with Lexis and Westlaw is always a plus.

Paralegal Analyst – Dept. of Legal Affairs, Hospital

Negotiate, draft, and finalize agreements; draft professional service agreements, patient transfers, real estate leases; oversee litigation-related document retrieval, analysis, and production; draft and arrange for recordation of deeds of trust, negotiable notes, RESPA documents; perform research and/or draft informational reports, memoranda. Prepare documents re real estate holdings, investments.

Respond to inquiries regarding charitable gifts, billing problems, fee structures, Perform legal and factual research and analysis. Create and maintain department files on charitable gifts, trusts, and estates; prepare quarterly reports of outside legal fees for executive management and directors.

What You Need to Succeed: Bachelor's degree and Paralegal Certification required. Notary preferred. Experience with real estate, corporate and/or probate/estates. Excellent verbal and written communication skills. Computer skills including spreadsheets (Excel), Windows, Lexis-Nexis.

Associate Paralegal – Microsoft, Legal & Corporate Affairs

The company advertised for an Associate Paralegal. Duties included providing administrative and basic legal support to attorneys, paralegals and members of Legal and Corporate Affairs. Draft, proofread and finalize contracts such as non-disclosure agreements, vendor work agreements, professional services and consulting agreements.

Other duties included: investigate complex legal issues such as patent, copyright, intellectual property, indemnification. Review agreements to answer unit questions about contracts.

What You Need to Succeed: The company prefers experience in drafting contracts. Proficiency with Word, Excel, Outlook, and PowerPoint. College degree or equivalent work experience as an associate paralegal or paralegal; paralegal certificate or J.D. was a definite plus.

Supervising & Managing Paralegal for ING Mutual Funds

ING Funds advertised for a Mutual Funds paralegal. The position required preparation of drafts of registration statements and supplements to the prospectuses for the company's mutual funds. Preparation of annual updates, new funds and new classes; EDGAR submissions for registration statements and supplements. The position called for an individual to supervise and assist in training of paralegals and schedule work flow. Additional duties included managing vacation schedules; financial printer relationships including invoice approval; and developing and maintenance of processes.

What You Need to Succeed: College degree or relevant experience. Paralegal certificate preferred. Advanced knowledge of federal securities laws and mutual fund filings and ability to train junior staff members in legal concepts of the securities acts.

Other similar employers: Banks, investment firms, law firms.

Employee Benefits Paralegal, Retirement & Welfare Plans

Support in-house benefits counsel responsible for retirement and welfare benefit plans. Preparation and review of plan documents and forms, including plan amendments and supporting corporate resolutions; assist with preparation of IRS and DOL filings; review and prepare correspondence relating to Qualified Domestic Relations Orders; maintenance of plan files; monitor legal and non-legal developments affecting employee benefit plans and compensation arrangements.

What You Need to Succeed: B.A./B.S. degree; paralegal certificate preferred.

Salary: $65-70,000 (3+ years experience in Baltimore).

Legal Services Administrator
United Health Group

This health care organization advertised for a paralegal with strong contract writing experience. The position involved negotiations with clinical staff, analyzing and drafting clinical study agreements.

What You Need to Succeed: Experience reviewing, negotiating and drafting agreements and contracts; within the field of clinical studies. Strong communication and presentation skills; and contract writing experience.

Paralegal – Marriott International, General Corporate Work

When Marriott International promised "a truly unique paralegal work experience" advertised online, the company did not spell out the precise duties of the position. However, the company described its paralegal professionals as "entrusted with a high degree of autonomy and responsibility, as they undertake a principal role in supporting the legal needs of our operations around the world and our corporate departments".

The organization's paralegals serve as a primary point of contact and provide guidance to clients in the field and at Corporate Headquarters. They resolve a wide variety of issues; assist in negotiating and drafting contracts and other legal documents; work directly with outside counsel on legal matters; and take part in ongoing Law Department-sponsored educational and training programs.

The company was named by *Fortune* magazine as one of the "100 Best Companies to Work for in America" and by *Washingtonian* magazine as one of the "50 Best Places to Work."

What You Need to Succeed: Highly motivated team player and self-starter; at least three years experience as in a law firm or corporate environment (corporate transaction or real estate experience preferred); certificate from an ABA paralegal program or qualifying paralegal experience; four-year college degree preferred.

Complex Claims Consultant for Insurance Companies

This position within well-known insurance companies is involved in a roundtable of files with senior management. This is an opportunity to leverage your workers' compensation background. Responsible for the overall management of highly complex claims. Work on highly complex investigations of claims, liability, compensability and damages. Determine if a major claim should be settled or litigated. Manage all types of investigative activity on major claims. Coordinate discovery and litigation strategy with counsel.

Negotiate highly complex settlement packages, sets reserves and authorizes payment within scope of authority, settling claims in most cost effective manner and ensuring timely issuance of disbursements.

Coordinate third party recovery with subrogation/salvage unit. Make recommendations on claims policy and processes to management. Analyze claims activities; prepares and present reports to management. Work with attorneys and account representatives regarding the handling and/or disposition of highly complex claims. Keep current on state/territory regulations and issues, industry activity and trends.

What You Need to Succeed: Bachelor's degree or equivalent experience. Professional designation preferred. 8+ years of claims experience. Learn new jurisdictions and experience in litigated claims and settlement strategy. Strong technical background with highly complex, high severity workman's compensation claims. Strong organizational skills.

Real Estate Director/Paralegal
Knowledge Learning Corporation, Chicago

The company sought a Real Estate Director with paralegal background. Duties included developing strategy for site selection and land acquisition for aggressive growth plan. Negotiate complex transactions for purchase/sale agreements, lease renewals and other real estate transactions. Partner with and direct the activities of real estate brokers, appraisers, assessors and consultants. Take responsibility for planning, organizing, and asset management of real estate portfolio.

Banking Paralegal
Northern Trust Corporation, Chicago, IL

Northern Trust Corporation needed an experienced paralegal to assist in research, preparation, review, and processing of legal documents. Conduct research for litigation using resources such as legal documents, periodicals, textbooks and other legal references. Conduct legal research. Review current and pending developments in banking laws and regulations. Prepare summaries of research findings. Process legal actions served upon the bank including subpoenas, court orders, and wage deduction orders.

What You Need to Succeed: The ideal candidate would have had a paralegal certificate and 2 years of course work. Organizational and analytical skills needed.

Senior Coordinator, Franchise Administration
Starwood Hotels

Starwood Hotels sought a paralegal for its Franchise Division. The responsibilities included performing multiple administrative duties in the licensing and compliance process; issuing and fully executing license agreements and related documents; keeping the franchise community abreast of all compliance-related issues; and inputting and maintenance of all franchise data in the database.

Responsibilities include accurate data entry of all elements of the license and related agreements into the database. Negotiate language in the comfort letter with the lender and licensees. Issue defaults, extensions and termination letters in connection with licensees not meeting system/license requirements.

What You Need to Succeed: Bachelor's degree or equivalent related experience; 2+ years of related work experience in franchising or the hotel industry or as a corporate paralegal (education level can be substituted for experience).

Legal Assistant
M.D. Anderson Cancer Center, Houston

Here's a very different type of position working for a Cancer Research Center in Houston. Conduct legal research requiring significant independent initiative, discretion and critical thinking analysis and judgment, examine, interpret and apply statutes, court decisions, and other legal materials in preparing routine legal documents. Research and analyze a variety of statutes, ordinances, court decisions, institutional policies and procedures, and articles for preparing reports and legal documents.

Monitor and conduct research of federal and state databases; schedule and facilitate training sessions, meetings and conferences. Provide assistance and distribution of materials generated by the Institutional Compliance Office, assist in collection of data and information for The University of Texas System, compliance risk assessments, quarterly newsletters, and new legal developments such as case law and agency guidance. Assist with quarterly newsletter.

What You Need to Succeed: Associates degree with 2+ years of experience in a legal environment; Paralegal Certificate preferred. 3+ years experience in legal research and investigation.

Salary: $40,000 - $60,000 per year.

Entry-Level Paralegal – American Transit Insurance Co.

American Transit Insurance Company sought entry-level paralegals to join their No-Fault Legal Department. The position called for college graduates and offered an opportunity to obtain both legal and insurance experience.

The job responsibilities included:

- Preparing pleadings, memos and other legal correspondence.
- Drafting discovery requests and responses.
- Analyzing and evaluating No-Fault lawsuits.
- Providing a Claims Review in preparation for motions and trials.
- Developing and recommending strategies for defenses involving coverage, policy violations and medical necessity.
- Coordinating and scheduling witnesses to appear for trial, including Claims Examiners, Medical Experts, and SIU Investigators.

Mortgage Banking Paralegal – Generalist Position

Provide customer service to internal and external customers. Respond to requests for legal services from the various sections of mortgage banking. Review wills, trusts, power of attorneys, deeds and various other legal documents. Respond to customer complaints; gather records and information and draft responses to mortgage loan documentation issues.

What You Need to Succeed: B.A., B.S., or equivalent and paralegal certificate. Experience as a corporate, transactional or commercial paralegal, or in a documentary/administrative capacity in a bank lending department. Knowledge and skills in basic mortgage servicing matters is helpful. Knowledge of Microsoft Office.

Director of Legal Services – Manufacturing Company

Here's a position in Van Nuys, CA that offers a variety of duties for those senior paralegals seeking to do a little bit of everything. Responsibilities include contracts administration, IP management and trademark filings, litigation management and discovery, insurance/risk management, corporate law, SEC reporting and state filings, international operations.

What You Need to Succeed: At least 10 years experience in a large/in-house corporate environment; excellent computer skills.

Salary: $95,000 - $112,500.

Perks & Benefits of In-House Legal Departments

Not all companies offer the same or even the same standard of benefits. It appears that in-house legal departments of corporations have most law firms beat when it comes to the variety of benefits offered. The following is a compilation of benefits found at several in-house legal departments:

- Medical and Dental insurance
- Vision insurance
- Life insurance
- Accidental death & dismemberment insurance
- Long term disability
- Short term disability (100% paid by company)
- Pension (100% paid by company)
- 401(k) plan (with company match)
- Paid parking (50-100% paid by company)
- On-site health club with showers (approximately $15 per month cost to employee)
- 9 paid holidays per year
- 2 paid floating holidays per year (used at employee's discretion)
- 2 weeks paid vacation per year (4 weeks after 15 years, 5 weeks at 23 years)
- Ability to buy an additional week of vacation
- 14 days of accrued sick leave per year allowed to accumulate over the years
- 7 days of dependent care leave per year (deducted from sick leave)
- 2 - 4 days bereavement leave upon the death of family member
- 8 hours volunteer time per year
- Salary is paid while an employee is on jury duty or military leave
- Flexible health care and child care spending accounts (using pre-tax dollars)
- Free annual flu shots provided on-site
- Paid professional dues
- In-house training provided
- Employee assistance program
- Adoption time off and paid expenses
- Unpaid time off if needed and acceptable to supervisor
- Service awards upon anniversaries of employment date (at 5 year increments)
- Annual bonus (depending upon performance of company and employee)
- Annual merit raises (depending upon employee performance)
- Legal services insurance (not a company-provided benefit but available at group rates)

- Paid infant care
- Home and auto insurance (not a company-provided benefit but available at group rates)
- 401(k) plan with company match
- Tax savings plans including Flexible Spending Accounts, 529 College Savings Plan, and Commuter Transit Benefits
- Tuition Reimbursement for degree program or continuing legal education
- Relocation Assistance
- Casual Attire
- Free lunch
- On-Site concierge services including dry cleaning, postage, and banking
- Free on-site fitness center
- Free on-site parking

A few of the benefits advertised by major corporations such as Google:

-Flexible work hours
-Maternity and parental leave
-Employee referral bonus program
-Employee assistance services for personal issues
-Adoption assistance
-Google Child Care Center
-Free shuttle service
-Fuel Efficiency Vehicle Incentive Program
-Onsite dry cleaning
-Coin-free laundry

Hot Tip

Those with medical backgrounds tend
to do well in the paralegal field. There
is an entire organization dedicated to
nurse consultants and nurse paralegals.
(SEE resources)

Personal Injury, medical malpractice,
torts, environmental, pharmaceutical,
biochemical, insurance, and many
more practice specialties embrace
knowledge of medical terminology.

It's not too late to incorporate
your medical background even if
it's from years and years ago.

Phyllis Costis
20 Year Veteran
IP Paralegal

Entertainment to Fortune 1000 Corporation

After starting her career in the typing pool at CBS Television, 51-year old Phyllis Cotsis has come a long way. Graduating High School in 1974, she started working and decided to go to Mercy College (Dobbs Ferry, NY) at night using her elective credits to obtain a Paralegal Certification during college. She worked her way up in CBS to the lower management position of "Negotiator of Copyrights" in the Columbia Special Products division.

Leveraging her experience in Copyright law, she decided to enter the legal field and got a job as an Executive Secretary to the senior partner in an Intellectual Property "boutique" law firm in New York City. While working there (and for the same person) for 17 years, her position matured into a Patent and Trademark Paralegal., something she embraced as the field developed.

Since it was a small firm, she was involved in all aspects including some litigation. "I was very lucky to work for a man who "took me under his wing" and taught me a lot", she says. "It was he who persuaded me to go to law school".

Beginning at Pace University School of Law (White Plains, NY) in 1989-1990, she again decided to attend in the evening while working at the law firm. "This proved too difficult for me", she says, "So, I discontinued this education after the first year (leaving with a C- average). It has been one of my toughest challenges so far. I still think about it but I did the right thing at the time."

One of the most fun times she had was at the same law firm. "I was asked by one of the corporate clients to accompany their office manager to London, England for a special project", she says. "It was a delicate matter so they did not want a lawyer with them, but since I was knowledgeable in Patent Law, I was capable of assisting with the project and acting as a professional agent."

After her law firm was taken over by a large New Jersey law firm and her boss retired, Cotsis decided to work closer to home. By then, she was married and lived in Orange County, NY. She was through with the 2-hour commute.

Gaining even more experience by working for another law firm in New Jersey specializing in Real Estate and Family Law, she was taught Matrimonial Law. Taking a year off to help her husband in his home business of patent drafting, she assisted his Patent lawyer clients. They generated computer depictions of the drawings and patent applications to the Patent and Trademark Office.

Four years ago, Cotsis was contacted by an employment agency she had registered with earlier. The job was working for the General Counsel in a corporate environment. "I began working at A&P in June 2003. When the GC left, I was asked to stay on as a Paralegal. A&P has gone through several reorganizations within the Company, but basically my responsibilities include overseeing their trademark portfolio as well as retrieving distributions from bankruptcies in which A&P is named as a creditor. "I am periodically given projects to research and prepare documents for outside counsel. I maintain and assign the influx of summonses and complaints. I assist and work closely with the company's Senior Vice President of Legal Services," she says.

How is the salary? "When I left Manhattan in 2000, I was making $62K. Of course, when I started working in New Jersey I was forced to take a very dramatic pay-cut. It was almost 1/3 of my salary."

The salary is not an issue. "I have no plans to return to the law firm", she says. "I really enjoy working the corporate environment. The office space and dress is less formal. The law firms are working for us. It is much less stressful. One of the reasons I like it is that I am always meeting new people."

Cotsis is practical about her career. "This specialty is unique in that it is not a good basis for transition, as is "litigation" for example, she says. "On the other hand, there are not many IP paralegals. That situation results in a greater demand."

When not working, Cotsis is wining and dining and going to the movies. "I also love to go shopping with my daughter and walking with my dog. I just learned to ski so we can do something as a family in addition to our summer vacations which are always adventurous."

Hot Tip

The Martindale–Hubbell Directory is an excellent resource to find law firms that represent specific industries and clients.

Go to www.martindale.com and search around identifying all sizes of law firms representing an industry you would most enjoy. Or, look up an in-house legal department, go to the corporation's website and learn how to apply for a job within that company.

If the company has a General Counsel but no paralegals, don't be afraid to pitch the idea. Convince them of all the great advantages to hiring a paralegal – specifically, you!

Chapter Six

Interesting Law Firm Careers

There probably has never been another time when so many opportunities have presented themselves for paralegals in law firms. With 7 out of every 10 paralegal jobs in a law firm, chances are pretty good that at some point in your career, you may end up in one.

With client pushback on excessive legal fees, the general public has become savvier as to how paralegals are utilized. With the trend for law firms to hire fewer associates, the level of sophistication of assignment for paralegals in law firms has been elevated over the past ten years. Combined with a never-ending drive by paralegals to keep upping the level of assignment, paralegals now perform assignments that were once only completed by associates.

One of the advantages paralegals have in law firms over corporate legal departments is that even with attorneys striving to pattern their firms after businesses, the structure still remains more fluid than those in a tightly-structured corporate legal department. Since law firms are still governed by committee and therefore governed by consensus of opinion, the atmosphere can sometimes lend itself to varying types of utilization of paralegals within the same firm. In some, each partner runs his or her own fiefdom, different from the next partner in the next office. This flexibility gives paralegals an opportunity to create and design their own positions. If you are not doing so, you might want to take the opportunity to start pitching ideas of higher level assignments.

Major law firms are actually the minority in structure of law firms. Most law firms in the U.S. have 10 or fewer attorneys. The smaller law firm has fewer resources and consequently, paralegals often have a broader skill set. A paralegal in a small law firm, for example, is likely to work on a case from its inception through trial. A paralegal in a large firm may only participate in the case once it has entered the discovery phase and goes to pre-trial, trial or settlement.

Paralegals in small and medium-size law firms usually perform a variety of duties that require a general knowledge of the law. They may assist in contract disputes, business litigation, family law, construction defect cases, real estate matters, wills and trusts, and other widely varied assignments. For example, they may research judicial decisions on improper police arrests or help prepare a mortgage contract.

Sole Practitioners

The biggest single category of practicing lawyers is the sole practitioner. They can be excellent lawyers and although no two lawyers utilize paralegals in the same manner, potential benefits and disadvantages of working for a sole practitioner include:

- A more direct one-on-one working relationship with the lawyer.

- Although not always the case, sole practitioners generally have lower overhead than a larger law firm. It is not unusual for a sole practitioner to charge less than a big firm might charge for doing the same type of routine work. Consequently, salaries may be lower than at a larger firm.

- Work on smaller cases. If you are tired of working on cases with 140 billion e-mails in discovery, a sole practitioner might be the way for you to go.

- A more informal working relationship. You are likely to get to know everyone in your lawyer's office if he or she is a sole practitioner. This can lead to a better one-on-one working relationship, which may make you feel more comfortable.

Small Law Firms - Two to Ten Attorneys or Two to Twenty-Five

In some communities, a law office with two to ten lawyers can be characterized as a small law firm. In a large, metropolitan city, a law firm might be considered small if it has up to 25 attorneys. The benefits and disadvantages of working with a small law office can include one or more of the factors mentioned above for a sole practitioner. Additional benefits may include:

- More expertise in a given specialty. In a firm environment, lawyers are better able to develop areas of expertise since they do not have to be all things to all people. As a result, paralegals may get an opportunity to specialize as well. Some small law offices are called "boutique" firms because they tend to specialize in a given area.

- A small law firm can handle a broader range of legal matters. Some cases are simply too complex for a sole practitioner to handle.

- Better coverage. No lawyer can be available all the time, so a benefit of a small law firm is having other lawyers and paralegals to help out on a matter.

- Pooling of knowledge and experience. It is always helpful on a complicated legal matter to be able to talk to other lawyers and paralegals to pick their brains. A small law firm is a great environment in which to do this.

Mid-Size Law Offices – Twenty-Five to Seventy-Five Attorneys

A mid-size law office would be a firm of perhaps ten to fifty lawyers in some regions and in major, metropolitan cities, this number would be between 25-75 lawyers. Potential benefits of hiring a mid-size firm include:

- Being the best of both worlds. A mid-size firm may have many of characteristics of a small law office yet at the same time have the legal resources to do battle with the big firms. The balancing process can be a difficult one, but many mid-size firms are successful in preserving it. Salaries may be somewhat higher in a mid-size firm rather than a small firm.

- Full-service capabilities. A mid-size firm may truly be able to provide more resources to better do your job. Just a few of those resources would include better technology and more secretarial assistance.

- Reputation. The larger law firms did not get big overnight. Such firms have usually been together for a number of years, and the fact that they have stayed together is evidence of a good reputation. Having a well-respected law firm on your resume can be a big benefit for your future.

- Contacts. The contacts that a law firm has may be just as important as reputation. Although it is not always the case, the larger the law firm, the better the contacts they may have, not only in bar association matters, but also the community as a whole.

Large Law Firms to Mega Firms - Seventy-Five to Three Thousand Attorneys

A law firm categorized as a "major" firm will vary in number of attorneys, depending upon the size of the city. Major, metropolitan cities may have law firms with over 1,000 attorneys albeit in different parts of the country. One of the largest firms in the world has over 3,000 attorneys. Some firms may be considered "major" but only have 75+ attorneys. It may be located in a city smaller than a major metropolitan area but large for the city in which it is located. Paralegals in small and medium-size law firms usually perform a variety of duties that require a general knowledge of the law.

Paralegals employed by large law firms, government agencies, and corporations, however, are more likely to specialize in one aspect of the law. Each law firm is different, each attorney is different and this is definitely a case of the firm's policy or individual preferences when utilizing paralegals.

What also distinguishes a law firm from other law firms is the law school from which the firm recruits. Major law firms tend to recruit the top 10% of the top 10-15 law schools in the country such as Yale, Harvard, Stanford, Princeton and others. These law firms look to hire paralegals that have outstanding academic credentials and backgrounds in other major firms. They also frequently require a B.A. degree and a paralegal certificate from an ABA approved school. Most of the firms will also require a stable work history.

A large law firm of fifty or more lawyers is still going to be able to do the same legal work of any of the smaller law offices. Typically, though, they have grown so big because of their ability to devote the legal resources and expertise that are necessary to handle large and complex legal problems. More particularly, potential benefits include:

- Lawyers with high levels of expertise who have been educated at the most prestigious law schools such as Harvard, Yale, Princeton, Stanford and others.

- Resources to handle legal matters for public companies, governments, and other large organizations.

- Clout. You are a formidable opponent if you work for a major law firm. It can convey a message to an opposing party that you mean business.

- Multiple locations. Almost all large law firms have offices in strategic metropolitan areas. More and more, these firms have offices worldwide. As businesses go global, this gives the large law firms a major competitive edge when it comes to representing international companies.

- Having an AmLaw 250 law firm (the top 250 law firms in the country according to *American Lawyer* magazine) on your resume can open doors for the rest of your career.

Examples of Law Firm Positions

Real Estate Paralegal in Commercial Real Estate

Assist attorneys in the commercial real estate practice team:

- Preparation, drafting and reviewing of leases and other collateral documents.
- Review exceptions to titles and prepare necessary documents to correct or clear title.
- Order/review survey and prepare legal description.
- Assist with Commercial Real Estate Finance documents

Salaries: $55-68,000 per year (Atlanta with 5-7 years of experience)
$55-75,000 per year (Los Angeles with 5-7 years of experience)

Paralegal Coordinator for Major NY Law Firm

Reporting to the Paralegal Manager, track daily attendance of department personnel; maintain the department's personnel files; prepare monthly departmental reports including staffing, utilization, P/L, vendor pricing, emergency information; develop departmental reports and guidelines necessary to streamline procedures; monitor paralegal billing and overtime; coordinate work room assignments and space issues, assignments and staffing needs.

Provide support to paralegal practice area managers; process incoming paralegal applicant resumes including scheduling and correspondence; assist with new hire process including room assignments, orientation and training; organize annual paralegal review and compensation materials; assist temporary personnel with timekeeping responsibilities and workplace guidelines.

Salaries: $75,000 - $90,000 (New York major law firm).

Litigation Paralegal Manager – AmLaw Top 20 Law Firm

Supervise the activities of up to 50 Litigation Paralegals plus temporary staff, litigation clerks, assistants and others. Manage workflow, assign space, conduct reviews, oversee assignments, assist in selection of vendors, interview and hire paralegals. At least 3 years of previous law firm experience including significant supervisory experience needed.

Salary: Can go up to $125K+ (New York); May also include a merit bonus.

Litigation Practice Support Manager, International Firm

Report to the Director of Administration. You need 5-7 years as a litigation paralegal. Provide support and leadership for litigation paralegals, secretaries and word processing including staffing, training, retention and practice standardization. Responsibilities include client service, human resources, workflow coordination, administrative duties, team management and professional development.

Salary: $65,000 - $80,000 (San Francisco).

Director of Practice Services, AmLaw Top 50 Law Firm

The Director of Practice Services is responsible for the day-to-day management of the Litigation Support Technology Center, intranet, extranet and portal initiatives, database development, and workflow analysis and automation in support of the firm's legal and administrative departments. Litigation Support responsibilities include database development and maintenance, imaging and coding, electronic discovery and vendor relationship and management.

What You Need to Succeed: Thorough familiarity with legal service delivery processes and models, law firms, technologies specific to the legal industry, the state and direction of generally accepted and emerging technologies, and best practices with regard to technology at law firms. A minimum of eight years of experience in law firm-related Information Technology support and management. A four-year college degree; advance degree a plus or equivalent experience.

Salary: Can go up to $175, 000 (Washington, D.C., New York, Los Angeles).

Bankruptcy Paralegal – All Size Firms and Solo Practitioners

Interact with clients by phone and in person. Gather documents and research information. Review financial and legal documents. Prepare bankruptcy petitions, document scanning and data entry. Handle ECF filing, and communicate with creditors and Chapter 7 Trustees. Work on Chapter 7, 11 and 13.

What You Need to Succeed: Bankruptcy paralegal experience. Excellent computer skills including MS Word and Internet research skills required. Familiarity with BestCase software preferred.

Personal Injury Paralegal – Mid-Size and Small Law Firms

This is a position that exists all over the country. It seems as though there must be thousands of Personal Injury Paralegals. A Personal Injury firm can handle small slip-and- fall cases all the way through catastrophic injuries. The cases can involve simple cases through very complex litigation. Salaries jump all over the board. Personal Injury positions do not generally exist in a major firm. Rather, they are found in Mid-Size or small law firms or with solo practitioners. Some of the duties: Manage and review medical records and answering interrogatories; summarize depositions; prepare briefs; interview witnesses; conduct factual investigation; assist with client interviews; prepare for trial; prepare subpoenas; locate expert witnesses; assist with complaint.

Litigation Paralegal Manager/Case Manager

Large, Mid-Size, Small Law Firms/Corporate Legal Departments
This position usually attracts an experienced trial paralegal with a minimum of 5+ years of experience in a large or Mid-Size law firm, including paralegal management responsibilities. This hybrid position combines trial paralegal responsibilities and running the paralegal program, including supervising and managing the performance of a team of paralegals, case assistants and docket clerks. Paralegal management responsibilities include: managing the workflow by assigning cases and overseeing work product, annual goal-setting and participation in the performance management process, coordinating professional development training programs and assisting with the hiring of new paralegals, case assistants and docket clerks.

This is an excellent opportunity for someone who wants to continue handling paralegal management responsibilities while also managing cases as a senior litigation paralegal.

Medical Malpractice – Litigation, All Size Firms

Knowledgeable in medical terminology, reading and interpreting medical records, discovery practice, identification of and research regarding expert witnesses and trial preparation. Excellent communication skills to interact with healthcare professionals. Prior nursing experience is a plus.

Civil Litigation Paralegal - Small Law Firms, General Practice

Civil litigation positions are found in all size firms. However, a small law firm generally deals with: divorces and family law, fraud, breach of contract matters, commercial transactional work, small business incorporations, and wills and estates. Generally, client contact is more prevalent in a small law firm than a large firm. Draft discovery responses and divorce intake documents, court filings, Westlaw research and docket management.

Case Manager, Litigation, Antitrust & Trade Regulation

Large, Mid-Size, Small Firms, Corporate Legal Dept.

Case managers assigned to large, complex matters handle extensive document management and supervision: manage document productions/inspections. Supervise summarizing and coding of thousands of documents. Supervise crews of less experienced paralegals, case assistants and clerical support.

Supervise paralegals especially discovery and trial related. Preparation of motions: statements of fact; compile and assemble exhibits; draft declarations; add factual and declaration cites; check factual and legal cites; and proof briefing. Assist in deposition/witness preparation: locate and/or interview potential witnesses. Prepare notices and subpoenas; prepare deposition outlines; assemble anticipated deposition exhibits. Attend depositions; summarize and index deposition transcripts and exhibits; analyze testimony. Arrange document productions.

Draft interrogatories, document requests or requests for admission or responses. Summarize/index discovery requests and responses and assist in preparation of motions to compel. Conduct factual research; summarize evidentiary/factual materials such as business, technical, medical and insurance records; prepare chronologies and "cast of characters;" prepare factual memoranda; review documents produced to recommend further discovery and investigation. Perform legal research: check citations and Shepardize briefs, research procedural rules of court. Organize computer support.

Assist in trial preparation: prepare trial notebooks; assemble trial exhibits; assist in preparation of trial briefs; assist with witness preparation; arrange/coordinate witness attendance; prepare charts/graphs; assist during trial; summarize trial transcripts; liaison between attorneys, clients, witnesses, co-counsel, other counsel and experts; conduct post-trial jury interviews.

What You Need to Succeed: College degree and/or paralegal certificate preferably from an ABA approved institution. Should have 10+ years' experience as a litigation paralegal including trial experience and supervision of large paralegal teams. Anti-trust experience desired. Knowledge of computer systems used in litigation support.

Family Law Paralegal, Small and Mid-Size Law Firms

Your primary role supports Family Law attorneys in all aspects of case work and litigation work associated with the representation of clients.

Assist in client matters beginning with the initial interview; draft Summons, Complaint and Pre-trial Motions; Interrogatories and Request for Production of Documents; Notice Depositions and Issue Subpoena's. Prepare discovery responses; prepare letters, arrange meetings and assist with telephone conferences; Stay in touch with clients, answering questions and keeping them informed. Working knowledge of dissolution, custody, child support and family law motions practice and discovery.

Health Care Paralegal, All Size Firms & In-House Legal Departments

This position involves drafting, review and negotiation of affiliation template agreements and complex contracts as well as involvement with HIPAA and Employee Benefit Plans. The ability to quickly and accurately conduct manual and computer assisted legal research on point and accurately summarize research findings is required. Respond to contract related inquiries and routine legal questions under the direction of the attorney.

What You Need to Succeed: Paralegal certificate from an ABA approved program. Working knowledge of healthcare law and HIPAA is strongly preferred. Contract drafting, review and negotiation skills are a must. Be able to multitask, prioritize assignments, meet deadlines, manage a voluminous workload and work with minimal supervision. Excellent written and verbal communication skills necessary. Working knowledge of Microsoft Word, Excel, Outlook, PowerPoint and Westlaw, Lexis/Nexis, Access, Summation, Concordance.

Criminal Law Paralegal for Small and Mid-Size Firms

Assist in all areas of crime: from theft to murder, white collar crime, conspiracy to sexual assault and criminal defenses from sentencing and appeals. Assist attorneys with investigation and arrest through the trial.

Securities Litigation – Document Management & Research

Cases involve government investigations including Securities and Exchange Commission ("SEC") inquiries and enforcement proceedings and National Association of Securities Dealers ("NASD") inquiries. You may also be involved in cases regarding special committees of board of directors and internal investigations. Duties include case and document management for securities litigation; maintain case calendars; research arbitrators for NASD rankings, client contact; prepare exhibits, notebooks and other materials for trials, arbitrations and mediations; conduct basic legal research; draft discovery requests and responses; deposition summarization; Shepardizing and cite-checking.

Products Liability Paralegal – Plaintiff and Defense

Assist attorneys in product liability claims involving over many plaintiffs and multiple defendants. Oversee the entire case file and successfully maintain internal tracking systems. Just a few of the cases can involve lead paint; respiratory protection devices; claims of silicosis and other lung diseases; diet drugs; automobiles and heavy equipment; kitchen equipment; and more.

Immigration Paralegal
Law Firms and In-house Legal Departments

Prepare and review non-immigrant and immigrant visa applications and petitions; research complex legal issues including US immigration laws, and provide information and assistance to clients and callers.

Prepare clients for interviews and draft letters; consult with clients and analyze eligibility for relief in immigration laws; identify appropriate laws, judicial decisions and legal articles; prepare written case notes; Proficiency in English and a second language is generally preferred, particularly Spanish, Mandarin, French. Proficiency in MS Word, Excel and Internet is generally required.

Salary: $32,000-$36,000 in smaller law firms. Higher salaries are found in larger law firms and in-house legal departments.

Trial Specialist
Major Law Firm

Manage logistics for Firm trials locally and across the country. Develop, design, implement, coordinate, prepare and set up satellite offices/war rooms for trial team members; negotiate contracts for hotel accommodations, war room furnishings (printers, copiers, refrigerator, microwave, shredder, office supplies, office furniture), short-term office lease, IT installation, network wiring, security access, telecommunication installation and all courtroom trial presentation equipment (ELMO, court director, screen, monitors, projector, podium, book carts).

Supervise war room staff. Direct day-to-day administrative activities including war room and trial site set-ups; monitor and manage vendor accounts; review and analyze trial site expenditures to ensure compliance with negotiated pricing structure and budget. Provide staffing for offsite war room; travel extensively to multiple venues to establish satellite offices; maintain business relationships with real estate brokers, courtroom personnel, hotel management, and litigation support vendors (couriers, document scanning, imaging, copying, EDD and large document production, court reporters, videographers, mock trial consulting firms).

Arrange and handle all catering and dining requirements such as price negotiation, ordering, and special menu requests; interact with attorneys, staff, clients, co-counsel, opposing parties, graphic consultants, jury consultants, and expert witnesses. Supervise Firm docket, trial log and trial calendar.

Salary: To $112,000 (Chicago major firm).

Workers Compensation – Plaintiff or Defense Side
Small – Mid-Size law firms, Insurance Companies, In-house Legal Depts.
Work directly with clients, either on plaintiff or defense side. Prepare Interrogatories, conduct factual investigations, draft pleadings, assist in settlements, and work with insurance companies. These positions generally do not pay top dollar and are often very stressful and demanding.

Public Finance – Municipal Bonds, Public Hearings
Responsible for first drafts of municipal bond documentation. Must know terms, conditions, rights and remedies. Ability to initiate first drafts of documentation for review by attorneys, prepare, attend, and assist with pre-closing and closing documents, attend to post-closing matters, and prepare and distribute transcripts to appropriate parties. Preparation of Form 8038 and Confirmation of Issuance for filing purposes; responsible for publishing Notice of Public Hearings prior to adoption of Bond resolutions; locating allocated volume cap from various municipalities to assist in funding of bond projects.

These positions are primarily found in Chicago, New York and San Francisco, although other cities do have some call for this type of experience.

Salary: $55,000 - $65,000 for six years experience in Chicago.

Additional Positions to Consider

Appellate Paralegal	**Insurance Subrogation**
Dispute Resolution	**Lien/Foreclosures**
Insurance Coverage	**Creditors Rights**
Insurance Defense	

Linda Potter
Saginaw Chippewa Tribe
Saginaw, Michigan

Working On the Reservation....Perks, Stress and Rewards

Situated about two hours from Detroit in Eastern Michigan, sits the Isabella Reservation and the headquarters of the Saginaw Chippewa Tribe. The Tribe traces its roots to three bands of Ojibwa Anishnabek know as the Saginaw, Swan Creek and Black River Bands of Chippewa Indians.

With current tribal membership at 2,754, the BIA 1999 Labor Force Report shows a 0% unemployment rate and no members living below the poverty guidelines. Hard work, dedication and outstanding success in gaming casinos have vastly improved the financial status of tribal members.

Linda Potter, 44, is a paralegal working at the Tribal Council. A dedicated paralegal, she is enthusiastic about her job. "I work for the Legal Department of Saginaw Chippewa Indian Tribe of Michigan," she says. "It is an unusual environment because it is comprised of both a government and commercial enterprises. Sometimes it's quite a challenge to work for both entities."

But despite their recent successes, the Saginaw Chippewa people face many of the existing social problems mirrored from mainstream society, including crime, substance abuse, illegal drugs usage, potential influence of youth gangs, child welfare issues, domestic violence and much more.

To get the job with the Saginaw Chippewa Tribe seven years ago, Linda answered an ad in the local newspaper. Her 20+ years experience and solid background in handling plaintiff personal injury cases, estate planning and some collections/foreclosure work helped her secure the position. Her strong educational background helped as well. "I attended the University of Great Falls, Great Falls Montana. I earned a Bachelor of Science in Paralegal Studies and a Masters of Human Services with an emphasis in Legal Administration," she says. Her education has paid off for her in this highly varied position.

Working in Tribal law allows Potter to utilize a variety of her skills and abilities. "I have a wide range of regular responsibilities in this position and also handle the crises in which my supervising attorneys always seem involved," says Potter. "On any given day, I might be called upon to draft consultant or employment contracts; review a specific Ordinance within the Tribal law and draft recommended revisions to meet the current Tribal needs; prepare litigation pleadings and motions; or prepare research memos on issues of first impression within Tribal Court jurisdiction. I have a wide variety of assignments.

"Much of my work is self-directed within the established parameters of the Legal Department. I am told what the end result of a project needs to be and it is up to me to determine how to accomplish that result. I administer our records, information and knowledge management initiatives in addition to my responsibilities."

Working with Tribal law is not easy. Potter has significant challenges. "My services are in high demand. There are currently 5 attorneys in our department and 3 administrative assistants, none of whom have any legal education or experience, nor does it seem any interest in learning any of the more legally oriented tasks that need to be done."

What about her greatest reward? "I sometimes fell I am still waiting for this," she jokes. Interestingly enough, what Potter likes most about her job is the somewhat unorganized and dysfunctional way the department operates. While other paralegals might bail out over the chaos, these challenges appeal to Potter's skills and abilities in addition to her sense of taking charge.

The salary level for her position is $25.02 per hour. She works 40+ hours per week and is considered an exempt management employee. Although she works a lot of overtime, Potter still has time to spend time with her family and share in their activities and interests. She also enjoys reading, writing and learning new computer applications. Her life is full, well-rounded and interesting.

Professional activities played a role in her career. However, time-management and prioritizing came into play sometime into her career. "My life was getting too busy to accommodate all of my activities, so I had to make a decision to spend more time with my family. I am still a member of the Legal Assistant Section of the State Bar of Michigan and an affiliate member of the American Bar Association but not currently active with either organization."

What advice does she give other paralegals seeking to get into her specialty? "Working for a Tribe requires more generalist skills than specialist," says Potter. "The priorities change from day-to-day and sometimes hour-to-hour. I need to have at least a working knowledge of many Native specific federal laws as well as litigation, contract drafting, research and administrative abilities."

And her next step? "Right now my focus is on trying to win a battle with rheumatoid arthritis that has reduced my ability to use my hands and wrists."

Hot Tip

Keep your resume to one to two pages at the most. Use white paper as dark paper does not scan well.

Chapter Seven

The New Compliance Paralegals
Hot, Hot, Hot

Compliance is a relatively new practice specialty for paralegals. Since the Sarbanes-Oxley Act was passed, corporations have a duty to audit and enforce internal controls. SOX has created many paralegal positions that did not exist as little as five years ago. The field is booming with new positions.

FGCU College of Professional Studies and Continuing Education has announced a new Masters Certificate program in Compliance Specialist.

The College of Professional Studies' Legal Studies Program in conjunction with Continuing Education at Florida Gulf Coast University announced a new graduate certificate program in Compliance Specialist. This is a one (1) year, post-baccalaureate graduate certificate course to educate and train people to be compliance specialists. It is rare to find this type of certificate program.

The Compliance Specialist Graduate Certificate Program allows students to utilize pre-existing knowledge and offers new courses in an interdisciplinary academic curriculum. Students will study the law of compliance, how to operate a compliance program, function within business organizations to review ongoing operations, conduct internal inquiries, review records and interview personnel, write reports, interact with regulators. The Compliance Specialist Program offers a uniquely designed curriculum not available at any other institution.

Compliance is best defined as internal control systems that, in real time, require that competently trained specialists view business operations and systems with informed skepticism. A compliance plan must focus upon areas of known risk, but must also review all ongoing operations, and be wary of problematic patterns and practices. A compliance plan's mission is to confirm that the entity's business systems are not in violation of laws, etc., detect problematic conduct, but, in the event that misconduct goes undetected, to also protect the company from crushing fines, penalties, and loss of public confidence.

Today's compliance specialist requires: (1) an understanding of laws, rules and regulations; (2) familiarity with business operations and systems (3) skills to interview, investigate/interrogate, review documents and write reports, and (4) the interpersonal skills to work with management, meet with board members, regulators, colleagues, executives, clerical staff and others.

All courses in the program will be offered via distance learning, accompanied by low residence periods (i.e. two, one-week, campus periods during the course of study in one course). During the on-campus sessions students will work with law enforcement and industry professionals, participate in clinical classes, etc. The fifteen (15) credit certificate course, consisting of five (5) core courses of study with no electives is much like an MBA or JD in law.

For these degrees there are no pre-required courses of study. No particular substantive knowledge or background is either required or presupposed. For the most part students seeking the compliance program likely will come from backgrounds directly related to the certificate. The curriculum builds upon student knowledge attained from several pre-existing courses. It offers related majors the opportunity of advanced coursework from several disciplines as it ties into many, diverse, existing programs of study.

Currently Christian & Timbers, ranked among the top 10 U.S. executive search firms and the Top 15 globally, determines what is referred to as a Hot Jobs list by having consultants interview thousands of global senior executives at Fortune 500 companies, as well as high-profile, private and venture-backed companies to determine top-tier hiring needs. From this data they formulated the10th Annual Hot Jobs report in January 2005. Christian & Timbers listed Chief Compliance Officers (CCO) as #3.

For more information, contact FGCU legal studies program coordinator Bob Diotalevi at 239-590-7817 or bdiotale@fgcu.edu.

Corporate Governance Paralegal Assisting Corporate Secretary

Work with day-to-day management of the Corporate Secretary, assist with all matters relating to the Board of Directors, SEC compliance and filings, corporate governance and financing transactions of a Fortune 1 - 1000 Companies.

Serve as liaison to the Board of Directors and coordination of support for all Board functions including: Preparation and distribution of agenda and Board related materials; coordinate director compensation; assist to ensure the principles of the Committee charters are met; review and update of the Directors & Officers' Questionnaire; assist in coordination of the Company's Annual Meeting of Stockholders.

Maintain corporate records, draft corporate minutes, resolutions, consents, certifications, bylaws, articles of incorporation; and research information from corporate records.

Assist in assuring Company compliance with securities laws, including Administering the Company's Insider Trading Policy; oversee updating of information in the Corporate Governance section of the Company's website

Preparation and filing of document with the Securities and Exchange Commission, NYSE and other regulatory agencies including Section 16 filings for directors and executive officers, proxy statement and non-financial 8-K's; Maintaining processes for Section 16 compliance; supporting corporate transactions, including financings and M&A; serve as liaison to shareholders, transfer agent, outside law firms, and vendors.

Where You Might Find This Position: Illinois Tool; Southern California Edison; Time Warner; Fortune 1 – 1000 corporations; public corporations; law firms.

Salaries: $85-95,000 per year (Los Angeles).

Insurance Compliance Paralegal
WellPoint, Inc.

An Insurance Compliance Paralegal sought by WellPoint is responsible for developing language for individual and group health policies and member certificates; file contract language with state insurance departments and pursue approvals; provide research and analyze state and federal insurance laws and regulations regarding medical products; provide guidance to other internal departments regarding compliance issues; maintain records and documents associated with these duties; conduct research on insurance laws and regulations; assist with implementation of regulatory requirements or regulatory audit recommendations.

What You Need to Succeed: WellPoint requires a B.A./B.S. and 5+ years of experience in an insurance or managed care setting, including experience with insurance filings and regulations or equivalent combination of education and health insurance company experience. Individual and small group health insurance experience including research of state insurance laws and applicable federal laws such as HIPAA and ERISA.

Marketing Legislative Specialist
Blue Cross and Blue Shield of Illinois

Very interesting position particularly for those who are seeking a very different challenge. Responsibilities include monitoring, tracking, evaluating, measuring the impact of legislation, participating in implementation and delivery of changes to our customers; and ensuring adequate internal review of policy enhancements or new initiatives such as Medicare products, Performance Guarantees, COBRA, HIPAA, and issues surrounding the uninsured.

What You Need to Succeed: Blue Cross and Blue Shield asked for pretty extensive background: Four -year degree or 4-years in a regulatory environment; 2 years experience analyzing and interpreting complex legislative, regulatory, or legal impact on business products, policies, and/or procedures; 2 years experience educating external customers.

Experience in working with legal staff and in negotiating complex legal issues; developing and delivering formal training; project management experience; knowledge of federal and state legislative processes and research vehicles; Medicare program, policies, and procedures; health care products; and understanding of principles of compliance, privacy and security.

Hot Tip

Always send a thank-you letter or e-mail following an interview within 24 hours of the meeting.

Any longer and you may appear to be someone who slacks off!

Raphael Beaumont

Corporate & Compliance Paralegal
Major Firm, New York

Hot Job & Major Firm
The Future Looks Bright for This Paralegal

For someone who describes his age as 5 decades and about 1,095 days, Rafael Beaumont must have some access to the Fountain of Youth. Loving his work seems to be part of the "secret formula" for this seasoned veteran.

"I work as a corporate legal assistant at an international law firm in New York City. I'm officially assigned to the corporate department, but as the firm's "official" evening paralegal, I have to provide assistance to the attorneys in the department and any other department if it is necessary. I consider this a very fortunate position because it gives exposure to all phases corporate practice."

Landing in the corporate specialty was no accident. "The corporate specialty is about finding solutions to your clients concerns and at the same guiding him/her/it towards a path of complete adherence with the law as it pursues it business objective," says Beaumont. "It is also about using knowledge of the law as well as diplomatic skills to arrive at an agreement."

Born in the Dominican Republic, Beaumont's mother moved the

family to New York forty-one years ago. Prior to becoming a paralegal, he worked for the City of New York Board of Education as a paraprofessional (educational associate), the equivalent of a paralegal in the public education system. "I studied hard in political science, criminal justice and paralegal studies at the Long Island University in New York.," he says.

Landing his current position through a professional agency, Beaumont's duties include preparing UCC financing statements, filing corporate documents, maintaining corporate minutes books, and other related duties.

"I started as a volunteer with a local lawyers' association during my high school senior year," he says, "and after I completed my paralegal studies, I spent several years working with various solo practitioners. This was a very interesting period in any professional life because I learned the meaning of "assisting a lawyer". I learned how to prepare "the first draft" of a legal document and how to do legal research. Although, the nature of the work is more substantive when one works with a solo practitioner, I wanted to work for a large international firm. So in 1996, I decided to pursue a corporate practice specialty."

Life in the law firm hasn't always been a rose garden. What's been the toughest challenge? "I have to admit that my toughest challenge has been learning to work with attorneys who think that they are the only ones with a brain," jokes Beaumont. The hours aren't exactly easy either but for him, it's just part of the job and part of the expectations of a major firm. "Working overtime is the norm when you do work in New York City," Beaumont comments.

However, the rewards have been plenty. "At this point, my greatest reward is receiving an invitation from a respected paralegal education organization to educate and motivate other paralegals. As a future professor of legal studies, I consider this opportunity the beginning of my teaching career."

Life for paralegals in New York City can be financially rewarding. "Especially experienced ones who make "comfortable" salaries," observes Beaumont, "But keep in mind the cost of living in this city is one of the highest in the nation." That doesn't prevent him from his favorite past times of enjoying chess games and absorbing himself in international affairs, however.

Beaumont is high on education, particularly for those who are seeking to get into the corporate specialty. "I recommend learning as much as possible about corporate law and practice by researching, reading, networking," he says.

Beaumont maintains his memberships in NALA, NFPA, ABA, and NALDP and on an advisory board for a paralegal program. A heavy workload prevents him from being as active in the professional associations as he would like. "I'd always like more time but there are only 24 hours in a day," he says.

His next step? "I'm planning to start advanced studies in the areas of regulatory and compliance as it relates to the securities industry," he says, "I'm planning to continue my corporate paralegal career and at the same time teach paralegal studies, preferably at a great university or at the college level."

Chapter Eight

The News on Contract Administration

If you don't enjoy the process of drafting, writing and redrafting, the contract administration specialty is probably not for you. Use of original language along with standard boilerplate, excellent word processing skills and lots of patience are required. Paralegals whose primary duties focus on contracts are most often found first within corporate legal department.

The ability to negotiate contracts from purchase, customer service agreements, licensing, franchising, distributor, sales, finance, proposals and more is part of the day-to-day responsibilities in this interesting and varied career.

Examples of Contract Administration Positions

Contract Manager/Paralegal
Model #1

Generally found within a corporate legal department, in this position, you will work with attorneys, paralegals, internal and external clients administering contracts, purchase agreements, teaming agreements, and more.

Prepare, review, negotiate and administer customer service agreements, hardware purchase agreements, agent and reseller agreements, alliance and referral agreements, teaming agreements, and non-disclosure, distributor, purchasing and other commercial agreements both domestic and international. Administer customer contracts and other transactions. Interface with corporate business units, Finance, Sales, and Customer Operations in connection with contracts and related matters.

What You Need to Succeed:

- Contract administration experience in a medium to large corporation.
- Paralegal certificate preferred.
- BS/BA or equivalent experience.
- Familiarity with and understanding of basic contract terms, structure, and operation.
- Drafting and negotiation experience.
- Strong organizational and communication skills.
- Database development and management preferred.
- Law firm or legal department experience.

Contract Administrator
Model #2

Review, evaluate contracts; purchase agreements; identify risk and cost concerns; complete and maintain Sarbanes-Oxley requirements; mitigate cost/risk through contract amendments; execute contracts; review customer bid requests; participate in proposals; process bond requests.

Temporary Contract Administrator
Model #3

Assist in the negotiation and drafting of the company's agreements with its customers and business partners to include drafting and negotiating license agreements, services agreements, work orders, partnering agreements and non-disclosure agreements. Manage a contract database.

What You Need to Succeed: Good analytical, drafting and negotiation skills and ability to prioritize multiple tasks in a fast-paced environment. Generally, a Bachelor's degree and three to five years of relevant contract management experience is required.

Salary: Up to $90,000.

Manager, Business & Legal Affairs Administration
New Line Cinema

New Line Cinema is the most successful independent film company in the world. The company advertised for a Manager, Business & Legal Affairs Administration. It produces innovative, popular and profitable entertainment in the best creative environment. In 2005, New Line partnered with HBO to form Picturehouse, a new theatrical distribution company to release independent films. A pioneer in franchise filmmaking, New Line's Oscar-winning *The Lord of the Rings* trilogy is one of the most successful film franchises in history. New Line is a division of Time Warner, Inc.

The company had a need in Los Angeles for a Contract Administrator in its Theatrical Legal Department. Responsibilities: draft, negotiate and administer contracts for below-the-line cast and crew members and all production-related agreements, complete insurance forms, manage clearance-related issues, and perform rights research. Additionally responsible for taking delivery of negative pick-ups and acquisition pictures, and prepare memos related to merchandising, consultation and approval rights, likeness approvals, advertising and marketing restrictions.

What You Need to Succeed: Prior drafting and negotiating experience; be organized and detail oriented, possess excellent written and verbal communication skills, able to work independently with minimal supervision, and ability to manage a heavy workload. Must have prior experience as a senior paralegal or contract administrator either at an entertainment law firm or motion picture/television company. Great career path!

Christy Stouffer

Practice Support Director
Steptoe & Johnson
Washington, D.C.

The Paralegal Executive

A star not only at her firm but in community theatre, a young 50 year-old Christy Stouffer lives the life of a busy paralegal executive. The Practice Support Director of the prestigious Washington, DC based firm, Steptoe & Johnson LLP, Stouffer manages all paralegals, project assistants, docket administrators, law clerks and a few other non-lawyer professionals for all of Steptoe's offices in addition to her other responsibilities and duties with the firm.

At the firm for 8 years, Stouffer started as a paralegal. "I had a number of other positions prior to beginning my career in the legal profession, including running a family-owned business and chairing a public interest group," she says.

Because of prior management experience and an expressed interest, Stouffer maneuvered her way up the career ladder. "I became a working manager after about a year, essentially building a tiered paralegal program from scratch," she says. After 11 years at my first firm, I moved to another firm to take a position as a full-time paralegal manager for two offices, where I inherited a mature paralegal program. Finally, I was lured away by my current firm."

Along the way, Stouffer took advantage of many resources to enhance her management skills and to promote the profession. The International Paralegal Management Association (IPMA) formerly the Legal Assistant Management Association (LAMA) was one of the most important resources available to her, and it gave me a wealth of networking and professional growth opportunities. She eventually became president of IPMA. "My presidency with IPMA was probably the most rewarding single experience of my career. I found networking with over 600 managers across the country to be inspirational, informative and enlightening."

How is the pay in that kind of position? "It is getting better as the profession matures."

Stouffer earned her reputation to the extent that eventually firms came to her. "My first paralegal position sort of fell into my lap after a partner at a major law firm whom I had met through a mutual acquaintance suggested that I'd make a great paralegal. After that, the jobs have found me," she says.

Not one to confine her activities to a narrow path, Stouffer enjoys teaching and public speaking. "I'm a former member of the Georgetown University Paralegal Studies Program faculty and a guest lecturer there, and a speaker on paralegal issues for numerous organizations. I'm also a member, former board member, former president and current committee chair of the IPMA and a regular speaker at the EstrinLegalEd Conferences." Any hint as to her next step? Stouffer is not shy about answering: "I'd like to be a management consultant when I grow up or retire, whichever comes first."

Hot Tip

Don't just think in terms of what you've accomplished as a paralegal. Moving forward into new positions requires leveraging your past careers.

For example, someone with a background as a policeman/woman might seek a position involving factual investigation. Make sure you leverage that background and get the $$ you're worth!

Chapter Nine

Unusual and Different Paralegal Positions

Paralegals are everywhere – where you least expect them to be. Listed below are just ten places that you've got to admit – who would have thought they hired paralegals?

1. Churchill Downs

2. World Wide Wrestling

3. Make-A-Wish Foundation

4. NASA

5. The Archdiocese of Los Angeles

6. Nike

7. Weight Watchers

8. Universal Studios

9. Sara Lee

10. Victoria's Secret/Limited Brands

Examples of Uncommon Paralegal Positions

Business & Legal Affairs Paralegal - Movie Studio

Assist in negotiations and securing talent and other agreements on behalf of movie studio. Review agreements and oversee clearances with respect to motion picture production. legal support for motion picture development and production including negotiation and drafting of agreements. Draft contractual language relating to ancillary products and rights.

What You Need to Succeed: B.A. degree and paralegal certificate; experience negotiating and drafting production agreements; working with SAG and Local 830 IATSE agreements. Strong drafting and negotiating skills, strong legal analysis skills, self starter, able to work under pressure; ability to prioritize and take initiative, strong attention to detail and excellent organizational skills; Strong interpersonal and analytical skills with a team-oriented and customer.

Where You Might Find This Position: Walt Disney; Buena Vista; Sony; Universal; law firms representing the entertainment industry.

Paralegal Specialist NASA

Work with the General Counsel of the Marshall Space Flight Center with responsibility for the analysis and evaluation of claims and other matters.

Salary: $52,355.00 to $68,066.00.

Federal Energy Regulatory Compliance Coordinator

Ensure that the [Energy Company] remains compliant with the Federal Energy Regulatory Commission (FERC) rules and regulations. Manage compliance training; Design and administer auditing process and assist with performing the internal audit; Assist with FERC compliance filings; Work with the company's FERC chief compliance officer, and external legal resources to prepare filings (such as rate schedules, tariffs, periodic reports) and maintain a record of filings including expiration reminders. Monitor Compliance Hotline Activity; assist in responding to, and documenting resolution of compliance hot-line calls.

Legal Administrator/Compliance – Television Show

You will monitor a live television show (Home Shopping Network) to ensure that claims made on the air are conducive with previously approved claims for that product. Attend training sessions for higher risk products and provide compliance training. Work with the show's guest and hosts to execute compliance program.

Criminal Justice Investigator/Paralegal
The Southern Center for Human Rights

Working for a public interest law office, your assignments include protecting the constitutional rights of prisoners and people facing the death penalty. Attorneys represent prisoners in inhumane conditions and practices in prisons and jails, and people facing the death penalty at trials, on appeal and in post-conviction proceedings.

The Southern Center for Human Rights is a vibrant office made up of 8 investigator/paralegals, 7 lawyers, an associate director, a public policy director, a development director, a coordinator and two organizers of the prisoners' families program, an office manager, two administrative assistants, and a varying number of student interns and volunteers.

The job entails travel to prisons, jails and communities to conduct interviews of clients and witnesses, obtain documents, and document conditions and practices in prisons and jails.

Salary: $30,000 with medical and dental benefits.

Paralegal in Hong Kong for American Major Law Firm

Skadden Arps advertised for a paralegal who is an expert of online research on databases such as Factiva, DJSI and Lexis/Nexis. You need to be an excellent proofreader and prior experience as a paralegal is as "distinct advantage". They also prefer fluency in Cantonese and/or Mandarin.

Contracts Manager
Bill & Melinda Gates Foundation

The Foundation sought a Contracts Manager with a paralegal background. The duties: Oversee the contracting process in the global development program, including development of business terms, finalizing contracts with legal, managing the contracts pipeline, and providing forecasts against budget. Work closely with program teams and members of the legal, finance and IT teams to streamline and improve the contracting process. Review proposed contracts. Identify critical issues (such as, legal, regulatory, advocacy, budgeting). Track pending contracts, forecasting contract costs and running variance reports. Develop system for tracking repeat vendors and typical agreements. Participate in annual budgeting process and manage the annual accrual process.

What You Need to Succeed: Bachelor's degree and a minimum of 5 years of contract management or legal experience. Paralegal certification is ideal. Experience in working with contracts, including drafting of statements of work, understanding basic legal terms, and basic budget analysis.

Medicare Appeals Specialist Working with Medicaid

Responsible for the research of all claims; assist with benefit eligibility determination. Summarize and assess facts surrounding each case. Draft final determination letters for all Medicaid beneficiaries. Research issues using federal and state laws and regulations coupled with contract law and any necessary additional sources.

Salary: $18.00 per hour (Pennsylvania).

Contracts Paralegal Administrator for Los Angeles Philharmonic

Highly unusual position for the Los Angeles Philharmonic Association! Music lovers seek similar positions! Prepare and administer all guest artist contracts (classical and presentations) for the Walt Disney Concert Hall and the Hollywood Bowl. Research and analyze law sources, legal articles and codes, and generally accepted business practices. Implement appropriate best practices and technology-based solutions in a cost effective manner. Report to vice president and chief finance officer.

What You Need to Succeed: Undergraduate degree or equivalent experience. Legal/paralegal training preferred. 3+ years' experience in high volume contracts administration; preferably work with music artist's contracts and other similar industry contracts. Strong proficiency with desktop computing, primarily word processing and calendaring/task management applications.

Belgian Competition Law Information Officer
Antitrust and Trade Regulation, Energy and Transportation Law

This interesting position caught our eye. The position required a paralegal to be part of a law firm's knowledge management team (Competition/EU) and work closely with lawyers in relation to a wide variety of cases. Monitor developments in the field of Belgian competition law. Knowledge of, and possibly experience in, sector-specific regulations in the energy, TMT and transport sectors.

What You Need to Succeed: Law degree or ability to demonstrate prior professional experience as an information officer/paralegal. Fluent in both written and spoken Dutch/French and English.

International Business & Cross-Border Transactions

Assist in international business transactions with respect to U.S. and cross-border transactions and related legal or regulatory issues. Prepare transaction documents. Support administration of international business transactions practice including preparation of minutes of bi-weekly meetings and updating important IBT references such as cross-border transaction forms files.

Prepare organizational state filings for business entities and maintain corporate records. Provide paralegal support for transaction signings and closings, and preparation of post-closing transaction binders. Create and manage due diligence data sites. Assist with marketing and knowledge management projects.

What You Need to Succeed: Experience as corporate paralegal preferred. B.S./B.A. degree or equivalent experience preferred. Paralegal certificate desirable. Strong communication (oral and written) skills. Knowledge of French and/or German language (spoken and written).

Corporate Paralegal – Weight Watchers International
What a terrific job to put you in the perfect surroundings to stay motivated to be healthy! Interact with corporate teams and clients to facilitate all aspects of transaction closings; handle general corporate housekeeping; maintain minute books and corporate records; corporate charts; prepare transactional board consents, officer certificates; assist in due diligence; review schedules to purchase agreements; assist in maintaining stock records; UCC/lien searches and prepare master logs; provide general administration and support; review all foreign packaging and advertising materials, all third party advertisements.

Trusts & Estates Fiduciary Accounting
Here's a position we don't see too often but trusts & estates paralegals are probably very familiar with this position. A 9-attorney firm practicing trusts and estates litigation in New York City was seeking a Fiduciary Accounting Paralegal. The paralegal would be completing fiduciary accountings and fiduciary income tax returns.

What You Need to Succeed: Knowledge of Zane Fast Tax fiduciary accounting software a plus but knowledge of other accounting software accepted instead.

Multilingual Licensing Paralegal for Law Firms & Corporations
Assist foreign sales force and attorney with a wide variety of matters. Manage transactions and client relationships. Assist with a variety of international contractual matters including software licensing transactions, Service Agreements, Vendor Agreements, Reseller Agreements, document preparation, as well as administrative tasks. Communicate with overseas subsidiaries on a daily basis, process translation requests which include setting up quotes with translation agencies and perform short translation and changes to standard contractual documentation.

What You Need to Succeed: Overseas working experience with (or in) Europe; experience at law firm or comparable in-house positions; Ability to work with different personalities, backgrounds, and temperaments; Diligent, strong and outgoing personality; Must be completely bilingual (English – Italian speaking and drafting abilities). French language skills a plus – Strong consideration will be given to trilingual candidates; Experience with Civil Law/Continental European Legal System a plus.

Salary: $45 - $55,000 (around 3 years experience).

Contract Paralegal
Microsoft TV

This position put you in a situation of mega-corporation and new technology. The duties included: Draft, revise and negotiate various agreements (including amendments and forms), such as licenses, technology acquisition, technology disclosure and services agreements; Review and analyze existing contracts. Review promotional, advertising, marketing, and packaging. Act as legal point of contact for client groups assisting in the resolution of legal issues. Assist client groups with the design and implementation of new policies and programs; provide training to clients and colleagues on select legal issues; Recognize/identify legal issues that require attorney advice and escalating them to the appropriate level.

What You Need to Succeed: B.A./B.S. degree; paralegal certificate; Internet businesses, consumer electronics, and software experience highly desirable; Contract drafting and administration experience; 8 years paralegal experience.

Trade Association
Washington, D.C.

A mid-sized financial-based trade association sought a paralegal to join its legal department. The position involved working on issues involving investor protection, preparing and editing briefs, and assisting with the correspondence and inquiries of the associations' members.

Salary: $55,000-$65,000 per year.

Paralegal Training Coordinator
Global Ethics and Compliance Team
Google

Recognized by Fortune Magazine as the *#1 Best Company to Work For*, Google sought a Paralegal Training Coordinator. Duties included assisting team attorneys in preparing regular status reports to the Audit Committee and the rest of the management team as well as assisting in the rollout of online and in-person compliance training for all employees and contractors. Responsibilities included organizing live training sessions by pulling in subject matter experts from across the company, and managing the localization and translation of all compliance policies and training materials and courses.

Just a few of the responsibilities included: Creating tests and feedback surveys to evaluate the success and effectiveness of Web-based and live training. Managing the code-of-conduct certification process and assist in investigations and code-related inquiries. Performing legal and online research on request.

What You Need to Succeed: The company requires a BA/BS degree with excellent academic credentials; At least 2 years of experience working in either an in-house capacity in a Compliance and Ethics department or for an e-learning vendor as a project manager or an ethics and compliance advisor.

Legal Specialist for T. Rowe Price, Baltimore, MD

T. Rowe Price advertised for a Legal Specialist to work under the direction and supervision of Price Associates' Sr. Legal Counsel to assist in the exercise, coordination, and maintenance of the Department's Global Investments.

Responsibilities: Separate Account Management. Prepare multiple separate account contractual obligations summary sheets, review contracts to identify provisions, may also include status of client agreements/amendments; client notification; client fees; QIB status; cross trade permission; IPO certifications.

ADV/Proxy Policy: Responsible for maintaining the adviser registration with by updating changes to the SEC registered advisers' Forms ADV. Prepare regulatory requests for the Ontario Securities Commission and other Canadian Provinces, Canada and Department of commerce regarding quarterly and annual foreign receipts and disbursements.

What You Need to Succeed: High school diploma, or equivalent, and a minimum of 2 years related work experience; or college degree. Self-discipline and tolerance for repetitive work. Detail-oriented and excellent proofreading skills. Excellent grammar and writing skills. Work well under pressure.

Hot Tip

Surveys forecast that by 2012,
e-discovery will be a $5 billion
industry.

No matter what your area of
expertise, you need to learn
about e-discovery.

It is not going to go away.
It's here to stay and lawyers are
becoming very, very
dependent upon your expertise.

Make sure you ride the horse in
the direction it's going.

Loni Morganelli

Paralegal
London, England

American Paralegal in London

If you have ever flirted with the idea of working abroad, Loni Morganelli is the paralegal to consult. Petite, vivacious and in love with life, this 25-year-old walking vitamin pill has successfully conquered what some of us only dream – living and working in Europe.

Sitting in her office, clad in London's latest designer business casual outfit, Morganelli graciously allowed us a peak at her exciting new life.

Tell us about your background.

Before coming to London, I worked for the law firm Cooley Manion Jones LLP in Boston, MA, USA for seven years. There, I worked in commercial litigation for the defense team. I was exposed to various case work in employment law, environmental law, insurance defense work, asbestos litigation, and property damage claims. I started out at the firm as a file clerk while in high school and continued to work my way up the professional ladder through college until I became a senior level paralegal. My experiences at CMJ set the foundation for my future, providing me with top knowledge and the best mentors in the Boston legal community.

With regard to my educational background, I studied Government and Paralegal Studies at Suffolk University in Boston. I graduated with a Bachelor of Science's degree in Government and a minor in Paralegal Studies. I achieved a 4.0 GPA in my Paralegal Program and a 3.6 in my major. After college, I kept up my legal education by attending Massachusetts Continuing Legal Education seminars, Massachusetts Paralegal Association seminars, and also participated in monthly online webinars in Concordance and Summation technology.

Did you start in another specialty?

Before starting at Herbert Smith, I did some work for a sports marketing firm. This was a truly great experience as it took me on a business trip to Dubai! My paralegal skills were exceptionally useful to me in this position as organization and attention to detail were of top importance. In this role, I was responsible for reviewing client contracts in media, publishing, finance and legal backgrounds and seeing that they were executed properly. Most rewarding, however, was helping to carry out a major business conference for the sporting industry as I had the opportunity to meet some of the biggest and most prominent stakeholders in the world.

Aside from this temporary position, I had always worked in commercial litigation. Yet again, I am now working in a new area of law, corporate.

What motivated you to work in England?

After working in Boston for seven years at the same firm, I decided I needed a professional change and a whole new environment. In order to enhance my legal career and increase my marketability and chances of working in a major international firm, I decided it would be wise to move abroad for some time to gain both a cultural experience and an international legal experience.

The year before my move to England, I began reading up on UK and European law, the professional legal structure in the UK, various law firms, and working requirements. I had always considered studying abroad in London during school but never took the chance. I felt this was the right time to make a move while I was young and flexible. I was also very attracted to working in the UK because of the generous vacation time and closeness to the rest of Europe for traveling.

What are the striking differences?

Living and working in England is very interesting. The pace of life is very fast, much faster than in Boston, New York, and Los Angeles. It is also one of the most expensive cities in the world to live in, which can make things a bit challenging sometimes. The standard of living is also much lower compared to America; however, if you are earning in the higher salary range, you can still live as comfortably as you would in America.

Public transportation is probably the most popular form of transport here as it is very expensive to own and drive a car in London. The working culture is also very different from the U.S. It seems as though offices are much younger and more relaxed in London, with employees getting together at least once a week every week for drinks after work. It is very common to wear jeans to work here too, as opposed to the more common business casual in America!

In terms of benefits, every UK employee and citizen receives national health insurance, unlike in America where insurance is privatized. However, both forms of insurance exist here, but everyone receives at least national insurance to start. UK companies also offer employees more vacation time with some firms handing out 25 days a year plus holidays. In terms of compensation, paralegals do not earn as much as their American counterparts, however, paralegals hold a law degree from their undergraduate studies. In general, paralegals commonly earn 23,000 – 25,000 GBP ($45,525 - $49,480) per year.

Most paralegals only work for 1-3 years and then they continue their education to qualify as a solicitor or lawyer. English paralegals also do not do as much intensive work as American paralegals. Here, paralegals are more apt to review and make edits to documents, as opposed to actually drafting documents under the supervision of an attorney.

It is very common for paralegals, however, to review documents and do some research, although in larger firms, they have research assistants (which in America, may be known as law clerks in some firms) to do that. In the UK, legal secretaries do work that is most similar to a paralegal working in America. While there are many paralegals working in the UK, the position is not looked upon as a long-term profession the way it is in America.

What are the similarities?

In terms of work culture, most people work 9:00 – 5:00 or 9:30 – 5:30 with an hour lunch at law firms. Employees are given pretty much the same benefits as in U.S. firms, except for the differences in vacation time and insurance as mentioned above. In law firms, the dress code is pretty much business casual with Fridays sometimes being more casual. In terms of the larger firms, it is common to find restaurants and gyms on the premises just like many of the larger firms in America. Overtime is also popular here among paralegals and in big firms, it is always available and compensated well. In terms of travel, similar to America, a paralegal is unlikely to travel with an attorney unless they are heavily involved in a case or transactional deal.

What are your responsibilities at your firm?

At Herbert Smith, my title is Professional Support Information Officer for the U.S. Corporate Team. I'm responsible for organizing and managing the library dedicated to US Corporate law and Security and Exchange Commission. I supervise three entry-level paralegals, also American, on projects involving this library. I also assist my supervisor, a Senior Associate for the US Team, on training seminars and legal programs for new associates, clients, and other firms.

What do you like best about your job?

I enjoy the vast amount of in-house training and continuing legal education opportunities available to me every month. The firm is very supportive of their staff attending such events and keeping their skills up-to-date. I also enjoy all the benefits of working for a large firm, including my generous vacation leave and gym membership.

What do you like least?

The only think I dislike at this stage is my commute. In London, all of the law firms are located in the East and I live in the West so it is about an hour commute each way on a crowded subway train.

What has been your toughest challenge?

It was really tough actually locating a position with a firm that would sponsor me for a work permit. In the UK, a citizen of the U.S. or of a country not part of the European Union needs to prove that no one else can do the same job or that only they possess the skills to do the job. As you can imagine, that can be quite difficult to prove sometimes.

What has been your greatest reward?

I love being able to travel around Europe and experience new cultures and people. There is nothing better than gaining an appreciation for another country's history and culture than seeing it first hand through your own eyes. It has been a wonderful learning experience and has given me a clearer, more open, intelligent, and informative perspective on the world.

How did you find your job?

I located my job through networking with the American Women Lawyers in London group. This group is great for contacts, support, and information. There are several paralegals and other legal professionals in this group and most of the women work for U.S. law firms which are open to sponsoring Americans for work permits.

What advice would you give other paralegals who would like to work abroad?

I would advise other paralegals interested in working in my specialty to do a good amount of networking and research prior to their move abroad. I would especially target US firms located abroad, or US Practice Teams in firms abroad. I would also advise anyone interested in working abroad to learn a second language, particularly French, German, Italian, Spanish, or Russian. Knowing one of these languages instantly makes you an attractive candidate and gives an employer more incentive to sponsor you. If it is applicable, I would also find out if you can apply for dual citizenship based on your family ancestry.

What do you do for fun?

London is a great city to explore so as you can imagine, I spend a good amount of time visiting new places, restaurants, museums, parks, and seeing friends. I love to travel, exercise, and cook, make floral wreaths and put together different flower arrangements in my home. I also enjoy reading, especially books covering topics such as current international affairs, globalization, politics, and fashion. My boyfriend and I also attend many soccer games both in England and abroad!

Are you active in any professional activities?

I'm a member of the American Women Lawyers in London group and a member of the Massachusetts Paralegal Association. I'm also an active member of the Estrin Legal Advisory Committee which I thoroughly enjoy, and I'm an alumni mentor for the Suffolk University Paralegal Program. I am very passionate about the law so having the opportunity to speak to aspiring paralegals about the profession is a very rewarding experience for me.

What's your next step?

After another year or two in London, I plan to relocate back to the United States and pursue a career in legal education and professional conferences or seek a position with the U.S. Government. I'm very interested in and passionate about the work that Homeland Security does to protect the nation against acts of terrorism and would love to help in that effort. I'm also considering pursuing a master's degree in event planning or possibly heading to law school in the future.

Anything you'd like to add?

With regard to working abroad in London, I think this can be a wonderful experience for the right person. If you are seeking a cultural, professional, and personal change, a temporary move to London could be the right choice. Living and working abroad is a very meaningful experience which is bound to leave you with a new perspective on life and a passport full of stamps!

On a personal note, I want to say how honored I am to have been included in this publication. I fully support the work that Estrin LegalEd does and believe that it continues to enhance and add prestige to the paralegal profession.

Chapter Ten

Leveraging Your Paralegal Background: Moving Within the Firm or Moving Out Entirely

Sometimes we reach a point where tough decisions need to be made about our career. You might be in a situation where you love the firm you're in but the work is driving you crazy. Or, you might be in a scenario where you can move horizontally but a move up a ladder does not seem possible.

In order to become and stay a paralegal, you are most likely above average in intelligence. Otherwise, frankly, you wouldn't be able to survive in the system. It is unlikely that a routine and repetitious job is going to satisfy you for very long. Now comes decision time: do you move up, over or out of your position?

By examining other job descriptions, it's possible that you may weave certain job duties and responsibilities into your present position. You may have to campaign to do so or your firm may be encouraging you to expand your horizons. Now is the time to leverage your background. Including those careers you may have had outside of the legal field. Everything counts in the legal field.

Go easy on yourself. You may want to move up but you might also be at a point in your life where making a lateral move is fine or even a step down in

order to "restart" another career. Be open to suggestions and do your
homework to satisfy yourself about what you want.

Alternative Careers Within the Law Firm or Legal Department Partial List

Accounting Manager

Auditing Clerk

Automated Litigation

Case Clerk

Chief Financial Officer

Collections Specialists

Contract Administrator

Data Entry

Docket/Calendar Clerk

Document Scanner

Facilities Manager

File Clerk

Financial Analyst

Human Resources Director

Knowledge Manager

Law Librarian

Word Processing Manager

Listed below are some interesting job descriptions. While these positions may not be the easiest to find, you may be in a situation where you can create the position.

Examples of Alternative Careers In Law Firms or In-House Legal Departments

Outreach Program Director
Law School

Develop and manage a comprehensive communication (outreach) program for law school including the maintenance of content of the College's web site. Coordinate and execute the College's message to its core constituencies, the courts and the legal profession, and to the public. Serve as staff liaison to the College's Outreach Committee and act as the national office liaison to designated state and province committee outreach liaisons.

Manage the web site content. Provide media and communications support for the National office, and designated State/Province outreach liaisons. Establish and maintain contacts with appropriate national legal media representatives. Develop and disseminate media kit. Assist in managing public relations agency and other vendors.

What You Need to Succeed: Four-year college degree or equivalent experience. Experience maintaining a web site, producing marketing plans and media releases, including providing content as part of an overall public relations/communications position. Experience working with national media. Prior experience in non-profit professional association or legal environment strongly preferred.

Law Firm Administrator for Small or Mid-Size Law Firm
Responsibilities are varied from firm-to-firm: Hiring and termination procedures monthly billing, transcription, train new employees, prepare daily reports, track settlements, preparation of correspondence, bill employee time, purchase office supplies, manage a small staff of legal assistants and paralegals, assist with procedures and various other managerial tasks. Previous HR or other management experience is generally needed.

Conflicts Analyst for All Size Law Firms
Perform computerized searches for conflicts of interest inquiries using LegalKey or other databases; open new clients and matters. Review for conflict of interest.

Secretarial Manager for Mid-Size or Large Law Firms

Coordinate and manage workflow of legal secretaries; act as liaison to attorneys and secretarial staff; coordinate training and orientations for new hires; work closely with HR Director with recruitment and staffing needs; prepare staffing reports; direct secretarial meetings; coach and employees; keep track of employee records, vacations and scheduled time off; direct and participate in employee evaluation process; assist with staffing.

What You Need to Succeed: Prior experience as a litigation secretary in a mid to large-sized firm environment, secretarial supervisor or management-level experience; excellent communication and interpersonal skills; experience supervising legal secretaries and coordinating workflow in Mid-Sized or large firm; ability to interact well with all levels of attorneys and staff; detail-oriented with strong organizational skills; Proven leadership skills.

Records Manager for Law Firms & Corporate Legal Departments

Oversee firm wide records management. Manage all aspects of the file opening and closing, including the management of staff, the development of departmental processes and procedures and oversee the records management system.

What You Need to Succeed: Bachelor's degree, and experience in law firm records. Strong leadership, management and communications skills with thorough knowledge of records and information management. Strong customer service and problem-resolution orientation with the ability to develop, propose and implement practical solutions.

Docket Analyst

This unique full-time position offers a qualified individual increased responsibility and expansion of their docketing skills in a variety of practice areas. Provide back-up to the existing Docket Analyst, manage and maintaining the Firm's docket calendar; enter and update docket entries, prepare daily reports, troubleshoot docket issues and provide support to legal staff.

What You Need to Succeed: Strengths should include strong attention to detail, excellent grammatical and language skills with consistent accuracy in daily functions. High School Diploma, GED, or equivalent required. Previous docketing experience. Preferred. Possess a solid general understanding of court rules.

Legal Trainer

Train on all Firm software and create training materials. Knowledge of Windows XP, MS Office XP and MS Office 2003 with knowledge of legal applications a must. Travel may be involved. Excellent Communication and presentation skills and the ability to work well independently as well as part of a team.

Marijuana Policy Project Campaigns Analyst
Minneapolis

Of course, this position needs to be aligned with your belief system. The interesting duties are challenging and different: Assist with legal research in all areas of state and local ballot initiative law, including signature gathering requirements, campaign finance laws, attorney general opinions, case law, and municipal codes; file all campaign finance reports; ensure that MPP's campaigns and initiatives comply with all relevant laws; act as the first point of contact and manage the day-to-day activities for activists who are on the ground in each of MPP's campaign states/locales.

Paralegal Specialist Indian Probate Cases
US Dept. of the Interior

Review Indian probate cases received from Bureau of Indian Affairs. Ensure statutory and/or regulatory requirements pertaining to Indian probates have been satisfied, the record is complete, and the case is ready for hearing. Search for and summarize relevant statutory and/or regulatory laws. Composes legal as subpoenas. Prepares case files for hearings. Monitor progress of hearings, assisting the hearing official in conducting hearings. Prepare draft Indian probate decisions as assigned by the judge. Compile reports required by the supervising judge, Chief Administrative Law Judge or Director, Office of Hearings and Appeals.

What You Need to Succeed: Two full academic years of progressively higher level graduate education, Master's or equivalent graduate degree (such as an LL.B. or J.D.). OR B. one year of (1) performing legal research; (2) legal/probate documents examination in order to ensure completeness and accuracy; (3) assisting the hearing and probate decision process; (4) preparing memoranda and routine correspondence; and (5) providing administrative support. OR C. Combination of Education and Experience: Education (must be graduate level or higher) and specialized experience can be combined if each is less than the required amount.

Salary: $45,878 - $59,640.

Knowledge Manager
All Size Firms, Corporate Legal Departments

A recent study suggests that US law firms invest less in knowledge management staff than European practices (www.almresearchonline.com). Knowledge management (KM) is capturing, nurturing and recycling the collective expertise of a business. In a law firm this means building up readily accessible bodies of standard documents, procedures, checklists and advice, so that duplication of effort is avoided. The study investigated 71 leading law firms around the world, 40 per cent of which will spend more than $1 million on KM this year.

Duties include researching; monitoring of on-line resources; assisting with internal journal updates; amending documents; assisting with presentations to new starters and reviewing/collating know how material.

Executive Director
Law Firm

Strong financial background to manage business operations including accounting, information technology, human resources, facilities and administrative areas. Highly developed leadership and interpersonal skills are essential, along with the ability to manage multiple, diverse projects concurrently. Significant participation in strategic planning activities for the firm, including proactively identifying process improvements within firm operations to increase efficiencies and effectiveness.

What You Need to Succeed: Excellent academic credentials including an advanced degree and proven executive and management experience and skills.

Office Administrator
Branch Office of Major Firm

Manage day-to-day administrative and operations functions, directly reporting to the Partners-in-Charge of the office. Work closely with the Executive Director and Director of Human Resources in support of Firm-wide objectives. Budgeting, accounting functions, facilities management and maintenance of contracts and leases, and management of the office's administrative staff, including support services, secretaries, paralegals, reception, information processing, information technology, library, records and training. Responsibility for the day-to-day human resources management, including compliance with policies and procedures, recruiting, performance management and performance reviews. Responsible for promoting and establishing a client service environment in support of the attorneys and Firm's clients.

What You Need to Succeed: Understanding of administration, facilities management, HR and purchasing. Experience with Mid-Sized or large legal or other professional services organization. Good interpersonal skills to maintain effective relationships with partners, attorneys, clients and staff. Four-year college degree in Business Administration, HR management or closely related field.

Accounts Receivable Collections Manager for Law Firms

Day-to-day supervision and coordination of Accounts Receivables. Monitor Staff activities to ensure timely contact and collections. Assist in identifying items to be collected and monitor activities during the month to achieve collection. Monitor accounts to be written off.

What You Need to Succeed: A Bachelor's degree and law firm collections experience at a management level and experience in budgets and supervision of employees.

Chief Operating Officer
Large and Mid-Size Firms

Manage financial, information technology, human resources, facilities and administrative operations. This position calls for a person who has had "hands-on" experience preparing budgets, analyzing and interpreting financial data.

What You Need to Succeed: Broad knowledge of computer and other operating and information systems. Excellent interpersonal and leadership skills, strong presentation and writing abilities, a record of accomplishment, be organized, willing and able to delegate, and capable of performing and managing multiple activities in an efficient, timely and cost-effective manner.

Salary: Compensation includes a very competitive salary plus bonus opportunities and excellent firm benefits.

Recruiting Coordinator, Manager or Director

Manage the associate recruiting and hiring process including on-campus and in-office interviews, and the coordination of orientation and Summer Associate Program and events. Oversee local associate professional development including Firm sponsored programs, CLE, and the mentoring program. Coordinate associate meetings and assist management in associate communications.

What You Need to Succeed: Dynamic and persuasive. Clear and concise verbal and written communication skills for effectively interacting with professionals at any level both externally and with the Firm. Proven administrative and organizational skills. Flexibility required to meet changing priorities, Confidentiality and discretion a must. Knowledge of best practices, sourcing information and commonly accepted standards of attorney recruiting, hiring and development.

Collections Coordinator
Large, Mid-Size and Small Firms

Oversee collections function. Work directly with attorneys to proactively follow up and resolve outstanding accounts receivable balances. Interact with billing staff in researching questions regarding payment histories and unapplied cash balances. Monitor status of bills submitted via electronic billing. Participate in annual pledge meetings and maintain database of year end projections. Use ARCS collections software and Excel to track activity and generate monthly statements.

What You Need to Succeed: Elite and ARCS experience. Excel skills required. Strong interpersonal and relationship-building skills essential. Ability to effectively work as a collaborative team member a must.

Help Desk Manager
Major, Mid-Size Firms, Corporate Legal Departments and Government Agencies
Responsible for the development of processes and procedures as well as leading a qualified team of help desk support staff in providing excellent front-line telephone support to in the use of the firm's computer technology.

Develop, monitor and improve the Help Desk. A few of the duties include:
•Assist with the design, development and implementation of a centralized help desk;;
•Implement improvements to achieve and deliver higher quality services;
•Track and analyze trends in Help Desk requests and generate statistical reports;
•Assist with the design, development and management of the call-tracking system, including project management and technical design responsibilities with respect to future migrations and upgrades;
•Analyze Help Desk activities; identify problem areas, and implement processes;
•Keep abreast of technology advances, trends, hardware/software products.

Oversee day-to-day activities of the Help Desk operations including:
•Evaluate, manage and direct Help Desk staff in providing first level support;
•Solve problems and makes decisions on a daily basis relative to Help Desk responsibilities;
•Assess and monitor skills, performance, quality, and efficiency of Help Desk staff and the processes and procedures in effect, and provide training and mentoring;
•Prepare and conduct performance evaluations, recommend salary adjustments and promotions, conduct hiring, termination and disciplinary processes;
•Involved in IT projects to ensure conformity across all offices;
•Meet with IT technologists, attend seminars and read industry publications to remain abreast of technology advances.

What You Need to Succeed: Bachelor's Degree; managerial and law-firm experience; functional knowledge of: Microsoft Office Suite (Word, Excel, Outlook, PowerPoint); Hummingbird DM; Relational database structures.

Work Flow Coordinator for Mid-Size & Large Law Firms

Provide coordination of secretarial workloads and assist or organize special legal projects and functions.

What You Need to Succeed: Experience as a Legal Secretary, Paralegal or Office Manager. Strong people and management skills and an in- depth understanding of legal secretarial work flow in a medium or large law firm environment. Bachelor's degree in Management or Business Administration preferred. Must be proactive, detail-oriented, and have the ability to promote team spirit and work independently or as part of a team; must possess excellent written and oral communication skills.

Marketing Director for Mid-Size & Large Law Firms

Act as catalyst between partners and the Business Development department for creation and supply of firm and client-specific brochures, PowerPoint presentations and attorney/group transaction lists. Distribute all marketing materials; Participate in meetings regarding conference calls for upcoming pitches. Follow-up with partners on client pitches and internal meetings - prepare notes, provide feedback. Provide marketing information for lateral recruiters, lateral candidates and new partners. Prepare spreadsheets. Assist lawyers in the development of marketing initiatives.

Assist in organizing on and off-site seminars, trainings, panel discussions and client meetings; Assist PR process; Track practice success stories; assist in appropriate efforts to publicize; Act as point person in coordinating the acceptance of firm awards and publicizing them; Assist in the participation in community programs.

What You Need to Succeed: Excellent interpersonal, oral and written communication skills. Ability to communicate with and gain confidence of lawyers and staff. Full understanding of needs and expectations of law firm clients. Ability to adapt to and work within the firm's culture. Highly organized. Ability to work independently yet stay within parameters of overall firm marketing goals. Ability to manage multiple projects while prioritizing work assignments.

Database Administrator for All Size Firms; Corporate Law Departments

Responsible for administration of all electronic databases and related issues at all locations. Manage and control data resources to ensure data integrity and security, recovers corrupted data, eliminates data redundancy, and improves database performance. Develop special applications and customized reports. Serve as primary support individual for all in-house developed databases and associated practice applications.

What You Need to Succeed: Bachelor's Degree in Computer Science or related field with database administration experience or programming work experience in database administration. Law firm experience.

Network Administrator – Internal Support & Integrator

Responsible for server administration. Build and configure servers, integrates applications and ensure that the network functions properly. Resolve system bugs and develop workarounds for existing bugs in network software. Manage Firmwide computer anti-virus program. Serve as the primary individual providing internal support for computer systems.

What You Need to Succeed: Bachelor's Degree in Computer Science or related field with network administration experience. Extensive knowledge of Windows OS Servers, desktop, laptop, and peripheral communications and computer systems. Understanding of standard desktop hardware and software as used in a window-based operating system environment required. Microsoft MCSA or MCSE and Cisco CCNA certifications a plus. Law firm experience.

Legal Secretary or Legal Assistant (Titles Interchange)

If you are looking to break into the paralegal field but are having some difficulty or if you are a paralegal who would just prefer to do something else, you might consider being a legal secretary. The position is also called a Legal Assistant in many firms, not to be confused with the Paralegal position. While this may be a "step-down" in some paralegal's opinions, it is a different position and if that is what you are looking for, this might work for you.

Some legal secretaries are promoted up the career ladder; others have trouble climbing it as some firms have problems perceiving you as a paralegal once you are a legal secretary. On the other hand, in smaller firms, the legal secretary might have a dual title of "Legal Secretary/Paralegal". If this is a good way for you to capture at least part of the title, you might want to consider it.

A civil litigation position responsibilities would include: drafting correspondence, briefs, discovery motions, and discovery responses. Coordinate conferences and attorney meetings. Schedule and coordinate depositions with court reporters, witnesses and other attorneys. Maintain attorney's calendar, prepare and file pleadings. Responsible for maintenance of file. Input billing for attorney and paralegal time using Juris or other billing software.

What You Need to Succeed: Excellent computer, grammar and writing skills. Position requires organizational and calendaring skills; knowledge of the court systems; good interaction skills; pleasant phone manner.

Salaries: $35,000 - $78,000.

Court Interpreter for State and Municipal Courts

Interpret oral and written communications from a foreign language to English as an expert witness in to introduce translations into evidence. Review materials translated with case parties. Certify translations made by others as to the accuracy of the translation; Review translated material for trial. Interpret for defendants, judges, lawyers, witnesses, social workers, probation officers, investigators, psychologists, state attorneys, and public defenders at pretrial conferences, during sworn statements, depositions, interviews, investigations, bond hearings, arraignments, the jail, plea bargains, motions, jury and bench trials, sentencing, probation hearings, domestic violence proceedings, court calendars, polygraph examinations, and landlord/tenant disputes.

What You Need to Succeed: Check each state and municipal requirements: Associate's degree or experience as an interpreter or any equivalent combination of education and certification. Knowledge of the types of judicial proceedings including arraignments, plea bargains, motions, and probation violation hearings and sentencing. Ability to translate and interpret fluently.

Human Resources Manager for Law Firms, All Sizes

Responsibility for all human resources management including recruiting, selection, training and development, performance evaluation, compensation administration, employee relations, motivation, counseling, disciplining, discharging, benefits administration, payroll forecasting/budgeting, workers' compensation, personnel data systems, job design, resource allocation and other human resource management functions for the legal, paralegal and support staff.

You may also be in charge of the supervision of facilities management, mail and messenger functions. Work closely with the firm's Board of Directors, Director of Administration or Executive Committee. The position works collaboratively with the Director of Accounting and Director of Automation to coordinate budgeting and financial planning, information and systems management, and records and file management.

What You Need to Succeed: Previous law firm experience is not essential. The ideal candidate must have a track record of success in human resource management and financial management of a large organization.

Hot Tip

Whether you are seeking to move to another
position within your firm; move up the ladder or
move out, think about who can
vouch for your good work. Who is
going to give you an excellent reference?

Start keeping "kudos" letters now.
Every time you receive an assignment
that says, "Great job". Save it. When you
can, get compliments put into writing.

If you don't keep your kudos file,
no one else will keep it for you!

Lisa Rosen

Entrepreneur and Litigation Support Consultant
Chicago, IL

From Successful Paralegal to Successful Entrepreneur

How would you go about describing Lisa Rosen? Spirited, funny, smart, witty, knowledgeable and hard-working would just be the start. Based in Chicago, the 30ish Lisa, a very litigation former paralegal with outrageously unlimited energy, left a cushy, high-stress and well-paying position at a major firm to strike out on her own in the area of litigation support.

It wasn't easy. There was the matter of having enough savings to cover her first few months. There was the culture shock of changing from a large firm environment to doing everything for you. And, of course, there was getting the word out - not to mention the insecurity of an irregular paycheck. But as a thriver, she was determined to be successful in her endeavors.

Lisa has taught as an adjunct professor in the Roosevelt University Paralegal Program, teaching a course she developed in Legal Technology. After working as the in-house trainer at Winston and Strawn for several years, Lisa formed Rosen Technology Resources, Inc. a resource for litigation support, imaging and coding, electronic discovery, software training/sales, and trial support.

Even though she has been wooed by major companies to come and work for them, she remains an entrepreneur. Working in the litigation support industry for several years she is certified to train on the nation's most widely utilized litigation support applications. In January 2006, she received the Law Technology News® award for Litigation Support Service/Consultant of the year for 2005. In 2004, she was awarded the prestigious Dataflight's Presidential

Circle Award for Outstanding Client Support and Product Development.

Leveraging her paralegal and trainer backgrounds, Lisa has provided consulting and training at several of AMLAW's top 100 firms throughout the country, as well as for in-house legal groups for many Fortune 500 Companies. She has also spoken before several groups about legal technology and vendor services

Hot Tip:

Having trouble trying to get enough litigation support training? Take webinars and seminars given by vendors to learn about their products and services.

That way, you can introduce new products and services to your firm or take the knowledge with you when you leave.

Chapter Eleven

Corporate Paralegals

Big Business Can Mean Big Dollars

Corporate paralegals are among the higher paid paralegals in the country. Why? Few paralegal schools offer a certificate strictly in the corporate specialty and fewer paralegals are actually in the specialty. While salary is an upside to the position, the downside is that the position is tied very closely to the economy. In a downturn or recession, the first layoffs tend to occur in companies or firms that are heavily involved in merger & acquisition activity. If you are not cross-trained in other areas, you may be headed for a bout of career inactivity.

Corporate paralegals (not to be confused with paralegals working in a corporation) are found in law firms and in-house legal departments. Their duties involve the formation and maintenance of corporations, subsidiaries, partnerships, LLCs and other entities. Responsibilities may involve assignments in securities regulations, mergers and acquisitions, due diligence, Blue Sky, closings, annual reports, working with Boards of Directors and shareholders and other related duties. The job may require fewer hours in overtime than litigation but when critical deadlines are concerned such as closings and mergers, you might find yourself working intensely and until midnight or more.

Examples of Corporate Paralegal Positions

Corporate Maintenance Paralegal - In-House Legal Department

Maintain and keep current all corporate organizational documents for U.S., European, Latin American, African and other entities.

Research and document business and other licensing requirements in fifty-state region and internationally. Work with government agencies to obtain and renew necessary licenses; Document and review applicable laws pertaining to uniform, shield and other requirements and assist with compliance; Draft and arrange for signature by authorized officers and directors of corporate entities all corporate resolutions, certificates, affidavits, powers of attorney, notarizations.

What You Need to Succeed: Paralegal certificate from an ABA-certified Paralegal Studies Program; skilled in the preparation of accurate, properly formatted and legally correct resolutions, and notarizations. ability to work in fast-paced environment with quick response time; strong computer skills. Proficient in Microsoft Word, Microsoft Excel, Westlaw, Lexis and database maintenance; excellent organizational and communication skills; high level of attention to detail.

Where You Might Find This Position: In-house legal departments of Fortune 1000 corporations; Inter-Con Security Systems, Inc.; Coca-Cola; Microsoft; Sara Lee; Neiman Marcus; public corporations with in-house legal departments.

Corporate Paralegal - Stock Option Plans & Compliance

Administer the company's stock option plans. Support the legal team with respect to all aspects of its corporate practice, including the coordination of, and preparation for, board meetings, compliance with applicable securities laws, support for merger & acquisition transactions, maintenance of corporate records and compliance with corporate governance policies.

Prepare, distribute, and maintain stock option grant agreements. Process stock option exercises. Enter new accounts, grants, and terminations. Answer employee questions regarding stock options. Prepare monthly reconciliations associated with equity.

Maintain minute books. Assist in all aspects of ongoing securities laws compliance. Coordinate legal department support for the Board of Directors and its committees, including the preparation and distribution of board materials, drafting resolutions, consents and similar materials, and assisting in the maintenance of the corporate records applicable to the Board and its committees. Perform other duties and responsibilities as directed.

Corporate, In-House for Fund Advisors – Regulatory Filings

Responsible for supporting the in-house attorneys. Assist with preparation of SEC, NASD and other regulatory filings. Maintain multiple corporate entity records, including corporate files, board minutes, and stockholder records. Coordinate and prepare board meeting materials for multiple domestic and international corporate entities. Assist attorneys with stockholder matters, including communications and meetings. Coordinate distribution of prospectuses and other disclosure documents. Maintain departmental manuals and procedures. Perform notarizations.

What You Need to Succeed: Bachelor's degree with 2-5 years corporate transactional paralegal experience. Paralegal Certificate preferred. Willingness to become a notary.

Transactional Corporate and Real Estate Paralegal

Assist the General Counsel in all aspects of transactional corporate law by searching, obtaining, compiling and preparing information. Assist with contract development, review and management. Assist in the creation and execution of lease and land agreements. Effectively and efficiently conduct timely legal research. Maintain and follow up with correspondence and filings. Set up and maintain data room for M&A transactions. Organize and maintain corporate governance documentation of company and its subsidiaries.

What You Need to Succeed: Generally requires an Associates degree or higher and a paralegal certificate; Corporate transactional, Mergers & Acquisition and governance experience; Superior data room organization; strong written and verbal communication skills; ability to work under tight deadlines and pressure.

Salaries: $50-$80,000 per year (Chicago, Los Angeles, New York, Atlanta, San Francisco).

Where You Might Find This Position: Acciona, Inc.; Kilroy Realty; Corporate Legal Departments that acquire other properties; developers; stores such as Starbucks or other chain restaurants.

Corporate Maintenance, SEC and Transactional Paralegal

Assist attorneys with corporate maintenance, SEC filings, mergers & acquisitions, formation of LLCs and general business related responsibilities.

Draft, review and analyze various contracts; perform contracts administration functions; assist with SEC filings, including Section 16 forms, corporate governance, intellectual property protection, and board of directors meeting materials. Assist in the preparation, maintenance and organization of all corporate records and minute books for the corporation and its domestic and international subsidiaries.

Coordinate corporate subsidiary filings, qualifications, incorporations and related activities with filing services and outside counsel, both domestically and internationally. Often act as the liaison between the company and outside counsel and certain internal clients.

What You Need to Succeed: Bachelor's degree; paralegal certificate; solid foundation and understanding of contract law; highly developed organizational, writing and communication skills.

International Corporate and Compliance Paralegal

Manage and maintain foreign entity corporate legal compliance on a global scale and providing support for international operations to ensure consistency across the corporation while minimizing business and legal exposure. Draft, review and approve corporate documents, such as board resolutions, powers of attorney, corporate charter documents, and inter-company agreements. Provide guidance to and manage external legal counsel on specific assignments, review preliminary advice and provide internal recommendations. Provide education to internal teams to assure conformity and consistency in application of business and legal policies and practices.

What You Need to Succeed: B.A. or equivalent experience, excellent academic credentials. Paralegal or similar experience with a top-tier law firm and/or in-house legal department, including significant experience in managing international corporate structures and compliances. Foreign language skills a plus.

Where You Might Find This Position: Corporate legal departments with foreign offices; major, Mid-Size and small law firms; Google; Baker & McKenzie; Paul Hastings, Janofsky & Walker; Kirkpatrick Lockhart; Fried, Frank; Caterpillar; Microsoft; Boeing.

Salaries: This position is on the high-end of the salary structure.

Corporate Securities and Corporate Maintenance

Work with attorneys and clients in preparation and organization of documents related to and coordinating closings of business transactions. Prepare business entity formation and maintenance; preparation of legal opinions, related due diligence and drafting related back-up memoranda; performing electronic research and obtaining documents from public and governmental agencies including the SEC, Secretary of State and Department of Corporations; experience working with attorney services in the filing and retrieval of business documents.

What You Need to Succeed: General corporate paralegal experience in a law firm or public company corporate law department. Excellent oral and written communication skills. Must be detail-oriented. BA or BS generally required.

Where You Might Find This Position: Major, Mid-Size, small law firms; corporate legal departments; Foley & Lardner; Cooley Godward; Akin Gump; Vinson & Elkins; Hilton Hotels; Wilson Sonsini; and more.

Salaries: Among the highest paid paralegal positions.

Securities Paralegal in Life Insurance Company

Supports attorneys in several legal practice areas, including individual life insurance and annuities, group life and health insurance, long term care, variable products, broker-dealer, agency, investments, banking and mergers and acquisitions.

Perform legal research on issues pertaining to the foregoing practice areas. Research federal and state statutes, regulations and case law related to the company's insurance, securities, investment, banking and acquisition activities, as well as preparation and updating of fifty state surveys of law.

Assist in document collection, organization and production, including company databases and document sources, in connection with responding to insurance/securities regulatory exams and inquiries. Maintain contract and office of the general counsel (OGC) matter files pertaining to agents, insurance/securities product development and distribution, investment management and banking relationships.

Preparation of SEC, state and other insurance/securities regulatory filings and related documents, such as SEC registration statements, prospectuses, annual and semi-annual reports, plans of operation and other periodic filings with insurance departments. Review and handle title and beneficiary inquiries and claim inquiries referred to OGC from various areas of the company, including the service centers, variable product service center (VPSC), AARP and group membership association department (GMAD).

What You Need to Succeed: Insurance and/or securities paralegal experience. Knowledge of Westlaw, Lexis, NILS, Microsoft Word, Excel and PowerPoint.

Salary: $55,000-$75,000 (5+ years of experience, New York).

Where You Might Find This Position: New York Life Insurance; MetLife; Travelers; Prudential; corporate legal departments of life insurance companies.

Additional Practice Areas to Consider

Investment Funds

Internet and Media Transactions

Mergers and Acquisitions

Financing

Securities Transactions

Joint Ventures and Leveraged Buyouts

Dale Proctor
Corporate Paralegal Manager
Washington, D.C.

Power, Prestige and Very Big Deals

E very day that Dale Proctor leaves her house in the suburbs and heads off for her job in Washington, D.C., she is never certain what unexpected exciting challenges she may be faced with when she arrives.

Proctor, the Corporate Paralegal Manager for Kirkpatrick Lockhart Preston Ellis Gates, LLP, a prestigious law firm with over 1400 lawyers in 22 offices across three continents is smack-dab in the middle of one of the hottest specialties in the country – the transactional corporate paralegal.

Proctor's workload varies from merger and acquisition engagements encompassing virtually all sizes and degrees of complexity. Clients have included publicly traded companies, privately held and venture-backed companies, partnerships, investment funds, management groups and entrepreneurs. Proctor works with the firm's clients ranging in size from emerging companies to some of the largest multinational corporations in all industries.

Her team represents purchasers, sellers, financing sources, management, and advisors in a wide variety of transactions involving both public and private companies, including equity and asset acquisitions of both entire companies and subsidiaries or divisions, mergers, tender offers, leveraged buyouts, spin-offs, recapitalizations, joint ventures and strategic investments. Assign Proctor to one of your deals, and you'll get a highly trained specialist, hard to find and in high demand across the country.

Proctor is one of the most highly sought after specialists in one of the hottest jobs for paralegals in the country. According to *Inside Counsel* magazine,

[March 2007] "There continues to be high demand for paralegals with four to five years of experience who are very technically savvy, particularly with e-discovery tools or who have a transactional background."

How does she balance a demanding job with family and a personal life? "I work very hard," she says. "But I always make time for my family. This job can require very long hours. However, it's exciting and I never know what to expect. I can work with entrepreneurial companies or large international corporations on any given day. It really keeps me excited about the job".

Hot Tip

Even if you work for the biggest
jerk in the city, it's a good
idea to follow 3
very important Do Not Rules:

1. Do not complain to future employers.

2. Do not blast your problem all over the Internet on listservs and message boards.

3. Do not write about it in your blog.

Chapter Twelve

Sizzling Intellectual Property Positions

Intellectual property paralegals cover trademarks, copyrights and patents. This is a transactional position, although there are many positions in law firms and in-house legal departments for IP paralegals who specialize in litigation. It's one of the highest paying paralegal positions available. Training is not easy to get as there are few, if any, paralegal schools specializing in the IP certificate.

Examples of Intellectual Property Positions

Trademark

In a large firm, you could work within the Trademarks and Advertising Practices Group that usually provides sophisticated and aggressive strategic representation of large and small clients in a wide variety of industries, both high-tech and low-tech, in trademark, copyright, advertising, Internet, consumer protection, and unfair competition matters. In a smaller, firm, you could work directly with one or two attorneys or within the Trademark Department of a large corporation.

The Trademark Paralegal clears new trademarks by gathering information from clients, commercial trademark databases, web search engines and other tools. You will review results for decision and/or attorney review; working with trademark attorneys and other paralegals to reach decisions and assist clients, the Trademark Paralegal reviews marketing materials for proper trademark use and assists in client education of trademark use and clearance.

Work with and manage and maintain communication with attorneys throughout the world in trademark prosecution and adversary proceedings; file new trademark applications and maintain trademark registrations before the USPTO plan and implement international registration strategies; and assist with review of trademark watch notices.

Patent Prosecution Paralegal – Patent Administration

Work with the Patent & Trade Office filing, administering and docketing patents. Extremely detailed position. Proficient with U.S. and P.C.T patent administration, including filing applications, amendments, appeal briefs, office action responses, restrictions, IDS, missing parts, assignments, ADS, Non-Pubs, issue fees, and many other USPTO communications. Pull together paperwork for filings such as Filing of Provisional, Utility, Continuation and RCE applications, Replies to O.A., prepare letters to F.A. requesting exam, and reporting letter to clients on the various filings.

Knowledge of foreign patent administration, USPTO rules, regulations and ability to research the C.F.R. and M.P.E.P is essential. Team spirit is a must; IP teams usually work closely together. Interact with a wide range of individuals on a daily basis, manage deadlines and work with attorneys, paralegals, engineers, inventors.

What You Need to Succeed: A paralegal certificate and/or college degree. Strong communication and time-management skills are a must. Knowledge and experience in electronic patent filing is a plus.

Salaries: Among the highest paid positions in the field.

Foreign Patents and Patent Applications Paralegal

Assist attorneys, agents and/or legal analysts in preparing and filing international patent application (PCT) documents and corresponding with foreign associates. Prepare, file, and docket Information Disclosure Statements (IDS) for U.S. and foreign patent applications. Maintain client IDS reference tables and firm reference library. Assist with creation, collection, and organization of client and firm files. Stay updated on laws. Meet critical deadlines.

What You Need to Succeed: High school diploma plus 2 years or more of related experience or equivalent combination of post-high school education; ability to organize business contracts, legal documents, regulatory documents, clinical documents, and patent and trademark documents. proficient with PC applications, including MS Office, docketing software, Internet software, e-mail.

Game Products Trademark and Copyright Paralegal

Here's a highly specialized position: Work with multiple studio and marketing teams to review and approve variety of materials associated with software game products. Prepare product legal notices. Review contest rules and prepare affidavits as needed. Conduct & analyze preliminary trademark searches using Review & analyze full trademark searches. Prepare trademark filings; creating records, updating and maintaining trademark database; Prepare U.S. Copyright applications & compile submission materials. Conduct legal research as needed.

Intellectual Property Administration
Live Nation, Beverly Hills, CA

Live Nation is the world's leading live music company connecting more than 67 million fans with performers at over 33,000 events and is the largest producer of live concerts in the world and the second-largest venue management company. Live Nation regularly produces tours for the biggest superstars in the business, including The Rolling Stones, Barbra Streisand, Madonna, U2 and Coldplay. Globally, owns, operates and/or have booking rights for more than 170 venues, including House of Blues-branded music venues and prestigious locations such as San Francisco's Fillmore Auditorium, Nikon at Jones Beach in New York and London's Hammersmith Apollo and Wembley Arena.

The company advertised for an IP Paralegal for Intellectual Property database management, including maintaining a complete database of the company's trademarks, copyrights and patents.

What You Need to Succeed: Strong written and verbal communication skills and the ability to conduct oneself with a professional demeanor in a casual environment. Microsoft Word, Excel, PowerPoint and Outlook software. 2-5 years experience as a trademark administrator or legal assistant in an intellectual property or corporate legal department.

Intellectual Property Trademarks Client Services Manager

Manage the docketing IP prosecution work exclusive to trademarks. master database, training, interface with IT on issues and developments, monitoring country rules. Assist with developing and changing trademark docketing policies and procedures. Assist with the management of staff IP prosecution support department for handling of the foreign/domestic docketing of IP prosecution matters (trademark). Manage workflow. Notify legal and secretarial staff of statutory deadlines.

What You Need to Succeed: College degree or paralegal certificate preferred. 15+ years of IP experience, thorough knowledge of trademark prosecution practice including docketing rules and websites for researching such rules.

IP and Anti-Piracy Paralegal Interactive Entertainment

Assist the Director of Legal and Business Affairs in Trademark and Copyright, Intellectual Property Licensing and anti-piracy matters. Negotiate and draft technology and intellectual property licenses, familiarity with legal research.

What You Need to Succeed: Experience in IP, extensive document review, organization and categorization in a fast-paced corporate environment. Undergraduate degree with a paralegal certificate or advanced degree.

Where You Might Find This Position: Sony PlayStation; Square Enix; Nintendo; other interactive game corporations and law firms that represent these companies.

IP Paralegal for Toy Manufacturing Corporation

Here's a fun position working with fun products: process legal documents pertaining to the licensing, design, manufacture, marketing and advertising of toy products. Opportunity to work with creative and imaginative people.

Draft and negotiate agreements and relating to the worldwide licensing of intellectual property rights from outside inventors, entertainment companies, and other entities; review products, packaging, advertising and promotional materials to ensure compliance with legal requirements; research product rights inquiries; summarize legal transactions and documents. Educate and train client group; work with marketing, design, finance and other departments.

Where You Might Find This Position: Hasbro, Mattel, and Leapfrog.

Invention Disclosure Management
Law Firms and Corporate Legal Departments

Manage incoming invention disclosures and coordinate with patent attorneys. Assist clients submittal of innovation disclosures to the Innovation Disclosure System (IDS). Respond to questions regarding disclosure process; maintain contents of Innovation Disclosure System (IDS). Serve as main contact for inventors/engineers, including monitoring and tracking of application process, obtaining information from inventors. Prepare and review patent application documents, Information Disclosure Statements, and other documents for filing with the US Patent and Trademark Office.

Docketing and Administrative Paralegal - Foreign Patent Prosecution

Manage the docketing for large U.S. and foreign patent prosecution dockets. Responsible for docketing incoming mail and patent filings using patent docketing software; maintaining mail logs; creating and assembling patent filing paperwork; scanning and archiving scientific notebooks; and providing general administrative support.

What You Need to Succeed: B.A. or B.S. degree is preferred. 5+ years' working experience, with at least 2 years' docketing and/or general IP experience is required.

Part-Time Trademark Paralegal for New York Firm

Prepare and file Intent-to-Use and Use-based trademark and service mark applications, Statements of Use and Extensions of Time to file a Statement of Use, Sections 8&15 Declarations, Renewal Applications, Assignments of Trademarks and Trademark Applications and Requests to extend time to file Notices of Oppositions as well as other common trademark pleadings. Good communication skills are needed as well as the ability to manage the CPI database of U.S. and foreign trademarks. Knowledge of foreign trademarks necessary.

Salary: $42 an hour.

Hot Tip

Work for a law firm and don't know how to switch over to a corporate legal department?

See if you can work for one of the firm's clients. Generally, both clients and law firms like the idea. If the firm is going to lose you anyway, it may as well be to a client!

Chapter Thirteen
Labor and Employment Law

Labor and Employment Law paralegals assist attorneys in discrimination, sexual harassment claims, age discrimination, overtime issues, unlawful termination and other labor related cases.

There are plaintiff law firms such as the well-known and respected firm of Gloria Alred in Los Angeles. Alred is the most famous woman attorney practicing law in the nation today, a successful advocate whose high-profile legal battles on behalf of victims whose rights have been violated have led to many landmark precedent-setting court decisions and hundreds of millions of dollars which she has won for her clients. However, the majority of labor and employment law paralegals are found in defense firms and in-house legal departments.

Examples of Labor & Employment Law Positions

Practice Support Analyst- Labor and Employment Law
Winston & Strawn

Winston & Strawn, a Chicago-based major law firm advertised for a Practice Support Analyst. This professional provides technical support and "know-how" to the Labor & Employment Relations Practice Group. The candidate was required to develop relationships with internal information management resources and outside vendors. Further requirements included developing a deep understanding of Labor & Employment Practice Group, including case team tendencies, workflows, and technology utilization.

Where you are most likely to find similar positions: Major and Mid-Size law firms; in-house legal departments; government agencies.

Employment and Labor Law Litigation Paralegal

Responsibilities include employment litigation and agency charge response support, including managing/supporting discovery, electronic discovery and litigation hold processes. Prepare position statements and information responses; handle statistical reviews.

Support non-compete and other restrictive covenant activity. Review personnel records, Prepare employment agreements.

Labor & Employment Paralegal
J.C. Penny, Plano, Texas

JCPenney advertised for a poised and professional Senior Paralegal to join the Labor & Employment group within the Legal Department in its Plano, TX headquarters. Work with a team of lawyers who advise the Company's management on all aspects of labor and employment. The work involves significant legal research, fact gathering and compliance support on equal employment opportunity, workplace privacy, wage and hour and other issues.

What You Need to Succeed: Ability to be flexible, multi-task, learn quickly, work independently and exercise sound judgment, handle multiple assignments and work directly with business clients, and will have excellent oral and written communication skills. The position requires a minimum of 4 years' experience in a comparable legal department environment or law firm, including substantial experience in one or more of the following regulatory compliance areas: Title VII, ADEA, ADA, FMLA, FLSA and workplace privacy requirements.

Hot Tip

Paralegals working for small immigration firms are in contact with the public on a consistent basis. While many immigration positions do not always pay the highest dollars, job satisfaction is high.

One paralegal who works in a major Atlanta firm enjoys her job immensely and earns an excellent salary. She prepares visa applications and immigration documents for sports teams, hockey players, jewelers, chefs, CEOs, computer programmers and other types of up-scale positions.

Chapter Fourteen

Fantastic Litigation Positions

Overall, there are more paralegals in the litigation practice area than any other arena. Despite the economy, litigation continues. In a good economy, more cases will go to trial as there is more money flowing and determined clients are more likely to pay for victory. In a down economy, cases tend to settle quickly, as clients do not have excess cash to pay for the long periods and hefty bills likely to occur just to get to trial.

Discovery Boom Continues

The proliferation of large-scale, document-intensive cases and the explosion of e-discovery show no sign of slowing down. Here are some staggering and sobering figures:

Discovery now accounts for 50% of the litigation costs of the average case, and up to 90% of the litigation costs in cases in which it is actively pursued (www.uscourts.gov).

- 90% of all communications now take place electronically, and more than 90% of all potentially discoverable information is generated and stored;

- A typical Fortune 500 company has 125 ongoing legal matters at any given time with at least 75% of those requiring e-discovery (*Corporate Counsel* magazine).
- U.S. companies spend an estimated $4.6 billion annually to conduct internal analyses of e-mail alone; e-mail analysis in a single, high-profile case can reach $5 million (www.law.com).
- Electronic data is obtained in 3 out of ever y4 lawsuits involving Fortune 500 companies (*The National Law Journal*).

What do all these number add up to? $2.8 billion, the dollar figure for discovery costs in the U.S. estimated for the year 2007. It is safe to say that with these figures, the need for litigation paralegals will most likely continue to increase.

Examples of Litigation Paralegal Positions

Litigation Paralegal
Corporate Legal Department

Provide litigation support, and assist in the resolution of escalated customer complaints. Maintaining database and files relating to customer complaints. Direct contact with customers, retailers, and vendors in connection with investigating issues and coordinating resolutions with multiple departments.

Provide overall paralegal support to staff attorneys responsible for managing litigation, supervising investigations, assisting in document review and production, preparing legal memoranda, and preparing for and making appearances in small claims court.

What You Need to Succeed: Strong PC skills with Microsoft Office (Access experience is a must, as well as Word and Outlook), Lexis, and Westlaw. A Bachelor's Degree and Paralegal Certificate from an ABA approved program is preferred.

Where You Might Find This Position: Corporate legal departments of customer-based retail, entertainment food, businesses; DirectTV, Sears, McDonalds, Caterpillar.

Litigation Paralegal
Law Firm – Complex Litigation

Oversee file maintenance and document production, review files, coordinate and work with practice support in the creation of case databases and extranets, oversee creation of database, input and/or manage data population into databases, manage court filings, supervise and participate in document production, supervise case assistants and entry-level paralegals and/or contract personnel, create and maintain privilege logs, perform cite checks, Shepardize briefs and other pleadings, search, retrieve, and update data and documents from Internet and various database programs.

Provide factual transcripts reference, conduct factual/Internet research, participate in substantive document review, organize and update case files and documents, coordinate document numbering/sequencing and reproduction using in-house or outside vendors providing such services, participate in document production or discovery requests, prepare charts, graphs, exhibit binders and exhibits for trial and deposition, organize pleadings and discovery documents, summarize depositions and hearing transcripts, draft basic memos and letters, may assist attorneys at trial.

What You Need to Succeed: Bachelor's degree. Paralegal/legal assistant certificate preferred. 3-5 years' prior experience as a paralegal/legal assistant in a large to Mid-Sized law firm with expertise in large complex litigation. Must have excellent computer skills including MS Word, iManage, Outlook.

Where You Might Find This Position: Law firms of all sizes; corporate legal departments; government agencies. Some examples: ThompsonHine; Latham & Watkins; Greenberg Traurig; Vinson & Elkins; Bryan Cave; Ballard Spahr; Blue Cross/Blue Shield; O'Melveny & Myers; Loeb & Loeb; Heller Ehrman; Preston Gates; Ice Miller; Kilpatrick Stockton; Wyeth; Department of Justice; Ogletree Deakins; Ballard Spahr; UPS; FedEx; Forfeiture Support Associates; Robins, Kaplan; Porsche Cars; Troutman Sanders; Orrick Herrington; Bingham McCutchen; Akin Gump; Foley & Lardner; Wells Fargo; Bank of America and thousands of other institutions.

Litigation Paralegal
All Size Law Firms

Provide organizational and substantive support to attorneys and paralegals in discovery, document management, pleadings, motions, trial preparation and investigation. Respond to discovery requests; attend document productions; perform document review and organization; index and make arrangements for copying or imaging; coordinate documents produced with document management systems; analyze and summarize documents.

Prepare witness files; select and assemble deposition exhibits; responsible for reproduction of exhibits; assist in preparation of direct and cross-examination; attend and take notes at depositions; summarize/index transcripts. Prepare subject matter/issue files. Monitor court docket sheets. Prepare issue files and document chronologies; assist in selecting and assembling trial exhibits. Prepare charts, graphs and other demonstrative evidence. Prepare pre- and post trial motions and briefs, including cite checking, Shepardizing and compiling appendices.

Provide support during trial Organize and maintain document management and retrieval systems, including computerized systems. Conduct court and docket searches, assist with manual and electronic filing of court documents and assist with legal proceedings in court. Conduct research and investigations.

Litigation Paralegal – Discovery Process, Trial and Post-Trial

Assist lawyers in all phases of the litigation process, from the discovery period through the trial and onto post-trial findings and appeals. Responsibility for document organization and production, including number-stamping, redacting, photocopying and indexing of documents, checking copies, setting up and maintaining files which are organized chronologically, numerically and/or by subject matter, stripping files at the close of a case; acting as liaison with the File Department in instances in which sections of a case's files or the entire case's files are maintained by the File Department.

Review and analyze documents for production. Conduct factual research: cull relevant information from a variety of resources, such as newspapers, magazines, libraries, case documents, trade associations, etc. Prepare for and attend depositions: gather documents relevant to the deponent, organizes exhibits; when attending the deposition, takes notes, photocopies documents, handle exhibits. Digest transcripts.

Prepare for and attend trial: organize exhibits, files and all other supporting documents; make arrangements for transporting and setting up files at court. At trial, take notes, handle exhibits, gather documents referred by either counsel, denote which exhibits are marked and offered or identified; interact with witnesses. Assist with the preparation of motions: pull relevant documents, proofread, assemble exhibits and indices of documents for table of contents.

Trial Support Specialist/Manager - War Room and Preparation

A Trial Support Specialist is a relatively new position. The position handles video depositions, exhibit and graphic support, and trial consultation. Set-up the War Room for Trial; Handle video, graphics, DVDs and trial preparation computer equipment and software. Assist with case preparation and trial and war room equipment set-up.

What You Need to Succeed:
- Associate or Bachelor's degree (Work experience may be substituted)
- Highly proficient with software (e.g., Outlook, Excel, Word and PowerPoint)
- Highly organized, detail-oriented, and self disciplined
- Excellent communication skills
- Work overtime
- Handle high-pressure environment, long hours and tight deadlines

- Manage multiple projects with ability to prioritize
- Able to travel
- Professional appearance and demeanor
- Experience with trial presentation software such as Trial Director, Sanction, LiveNote, Concordance, iPro, Summation and experience with Adobe Illustrator and Adobe Photoshop

Family Law Paralegal
Pleasanton, CA

Here's an example of a law firm position dealing with complex family law cases. The position pays well and is located in Northern California.

Responsible for:
- Serving as a liaison to the client and attorney
- Draft pleadings and correspondence; prepare disclosures
- Calendaring
- Legal research

What You Need to Succeed: Paralegal certificate; at least 5 years experience; experience attending hearings with lawyer; must be professional and detailed oriented.

Salary: $75,000 - $85,000.

Litigation Paralegal
Paralegal Association Advocate
Denver, Colorado

Rocky Mountain Paralegal

Litigation paralegals working in major law firms rarely have time to waste. Ask Debra Hindin-King, RP from Denver, Colorado. This 50ish paralegal icon works in a large full-service law firm with 13 offices; 350+ attorneys and is the firm's go-to person for general case management, discovery requests, depositions, trial preparation and research. A lover of travel, photography and gardening, Debra spends much of her time assisting well-known trial lawyers and high-profile clients.

Starting out with a B.A. Music and an M.M.E. (Master's Degree in Music Education); Debra became an Instrumental Music Education Teacher for 4 years. She switched careers to become a Petroleum Landman: a person who does contract negotiations, performs title curative, conducts due diligence, researches leasehold interest for the determination of oil and gas royalties and drilling oil and gas wells.

"My next move was as a Deputy Clerk at the U.S. Bankruptcy Court in Denver for three years," she says. "From there, I started as a litigation paralegal at Faegre & Benson LLP in Denver and stayed there for 9 years."

Employed in her current position for 9 years as a Litigation Paralegal at Holland & Hart LLP in Denver, Debra enjoys the challenges of a major firm. "I'm a litigation paralegal," she says. "I am also the liaison between attorney and client, general case management, review and respond to discovery requests, scheduling of depositions, trial preparation and subject matter research."

With all her years of experience, Debra says her biggest challenge is time management. She is in the enviable position of having to decline work assignments due to existing heavy caseload. "But my greatest reward," she says, "is being a valued member of legal team during the process of delivering services to clients." Debra has an opportunity to market her employment at the firm through public speaking engagements at CLEs and membership and leadership roles within professional organizations, a part of her job she thoroughly enjoys.

What advice would she give other paralegals seeking to get into your specialty or work outside the U.S.? "For those seeking employment in specialty: 1) Savvy with technology; 2) Knowledgeable about the local, state and federal court rules; 3) Flexibility with schedule; 4) Able to work independently with minimal supervision but also good team player in large cases; 4) Accept criticism with a positive spirit and 5) If necessary request clarification related to instructions for a specific task instead of wasting time and not meeting a deadline."

Extremely active in the Rocky Mountain Paralegal Association as past President and NFPA Primary and Secondary Rep, Debra has strong feelings about the value of belonging to associations. "Professional activities have assisted my career, says Debra. I have a tremendous networking opportunity with paralegals with similar career paths. The time has strengthened my leadership and communication skills and I believe I am seen as a more valued professional in the legal community and throughout the U.S."

Her professional activities background is impressive: She is Board Member, Chair and Region II Director for the National Federation of Paralegal Associations; an Associate Member, Colorado Bar Association; Member, Zonta Club International (Professional business women's service organization); and Board Member - Central Visitation Program (low income families that have been ordered by the Court to have supervised visits with non-custodial parents).

"But," she cautions, "Professional activities have sometimes hindered my career by limiting free time with my family and pet."

She is not shy about her next step. "Strengthening and re-evaluating my core values of my strategic plan to be a more prominent and respected paralegal in my community. I enjoy being a frequent guest speaker at CLEs. There, I share and learn from others about resources available to access to allow me to grow within the profession."

Debra Hindin-King words of wisdom for all paralegals? "Set realistic goals and expectations for yourself. Don't be afraid to cross-train in an area that you are unfamiliar with - great way to meet and work with a different legal team."

Chapter Fifteen

New Careers in Teaching Paralegal Studies

Teaching other paralegals can be a wonderfully rewarding career. Teaching jobs are not known to pay extremely well, however, the job satisfaction is high and the stress is usually low. Downsides to teaching are limited funding, cutbacks and the economy. Interestingly, admissions tend to increase in paralegals schools during a recession as many people have been laid-off and are seeking retraining or entry into a new career.

Examples of Teaching Positions

Faculty Member and Instructor for Paralegal Program

Teach undergraduate or post-graduate courses in the foundation areas of legal research, legal writing, civil litigation and ethics.

You might teach a legal specialty courses such as family law, real estate law, tort law, criminal law, estate law, business organizations, bankruptcy, employment law, workers compensation, contracts, & intellectual property. Serves as an Academic/Career Advisor and performs Institutional Service.

The position is usually a 9-month teaching position. Responsible for instruction; in several courses during the Fall and Spring Sessions. Day, evening, and/or weekend responsibilities.

What You Need to Succeed: Some schools require a Juris Doctor's degree. Others require a paralegal certificate or significant years as a practicing paralegal, work experience. Some schools require teaching background, preferably in higher education. Flexibility to teach in both the traditional on campus format and the online format. Excellent communication & interpersonal skills. Strong project/time management and organizational skills. Proficiency in Microsoft Office Suite, database management, and legal technology resources.

Where You Might Find This Position: Schools with Paralegal Studies programs in community college; four-year universities; vocational schools; online programs; certificate programs. Check out the American Bar Association's list of paralegal schools or the American Association for Paralegal Education (AAfPE) for a list of schools in your region.

Salary: Full-time instructors: $30,000 - $90,000 (top dollar is for head of program, Los Angeles).

Legal Assistant
Colorado Penal Institution

A Colorado penal institution posted a position for a Legal Assistant to supervise and instruct inmates, inmate law clerks and assist staff regarding the use of legal materials and the selection and preparation of legal documents. In this position, you will provide comprehensive and current legal material to Colorado penal institutions law libraries. Supervise operations and oversee the security of law libraries to maintain a secure work environment within a penal setting; and acts as liaison for inmates, and staff. Provide assistance and support for the office of correctional legal services to include duties associated with ADA issues, discovery, litigation management, offender grievances.

What You Need to Succeed: Graduation from an accredited college or university with a Bachelor's degree and a Paralegal Certificate obtained through a paralegal studies program approved by the ABA or from an accredited college or university. Substitutions: Work experience in the legal services field which provided the same kind, amount and level of knowledge acquired in the required education may substitute for the degree on a year-for-year basis.

Instructor
Paralegal Program, Hawaii

Hawaii Community College and The Center for Legal Studies, Inc., hires an attorney or paralegal to teach its Paralegal Certificate Course. The class meets Saturdays and Sundays for 5 weeks.

HCC has offered its Paralegal Certificate Course© since 1980, and there are currently 600 colleges and universities that offer the course on either a "live lecture" or online basis. The college takes great pride in its curriculum and instructors, and adheres to the highest standards of ethics and academic rigor.

As an instructor, you are provided with a complete set of books, a class syllabus, all tests, answer sheets, and instructor manuals. Pay is based on the number of students in the class.

Hot Tip

The bottom-line to accepting a job or a promotion is that there is no bottom-line. What is right for one person is wrong for the next.

Listen to your gut. If it's telling you not to take the job, there's probably something there. If this isn't the right position for you, most likely, it's not the end of the world.

It's much easier to turn a job down than it is to leave a job you're already in. If the job isn't right for you, employers would much rather you turned it down then to start it and be miserable.

Remember the old adage: Just because they asked you to dance, doesn't mean you have to dance!

Leslie McKesson

Paralegal Technology Coordinator
Western Piedmont Community College
Morganton, North Carolina

Hallelujah! Praise the
Singing Paralegal Program Director

Leslie McKesson, 48, is a beautiful, smart and very active paralegal educator. Based in North Carolina, she turned a paralegal career into a very rewarding and satisfying position by starting as a paralegal instructor and climbing the academia ladder to Program Director for a prestigious paralegal studies program.

You have a very unusual title. What kind of work do you do?
I am employed by Western Piedmont Community College in Morganton, North Carolina as the Paralegal Technology Coordinator (Program Director) and Instructor.

What did you do before your present position? Tell us about your background.
I was a legal services paralegal representing clients in various administrative hearings (Social Security and public benefits, direct representation) for eight years and I served as a Community Educator. I have also been a paralegal instructor for 18 years, 13 as a program director.

You must be very educated.
I have a Bachelor's Degree in Criminal Justice from the University of North Carolina at Chapel Hill, NC and a Certificate (Litigation Specialist) from the

National Center for Paralegal Training, Atlanta, GA, an ABA approved program. I also hold a Master of Arts degree in Leadership and Higher Education from Appalachian State University, Boone, NC.

I am currently pursuing Educational Specialist degree in Adult Education at Appalachian State University, Boone, NC.

What does a Paralegal Technology Coordinator and Program Director do?

I am a full-time instructor and the program administrator for the paralegal technology associates degree. This involves teaching a variety of legal courses and running the paralegal department (hiring and supervising adjunct faculty, budget planning and implementation, strategic and program planning, etc.) I am also an academic advisor assisting students as they prepare for graduation, and I advise our campus paralegal association. Our degree is available both on campus and online. I teach seated and internet courses.

What do you like best about your job?

The freedom to create new ideas.

Of course, we're going to ask what you like the least about your position.

The lack of resources (time and funding) to implement new ideas.

This position must have had some very tough challenges over the years.

Time and resources are my biggest challenges. Limited funding for additional faculty translates into larger demands on the limited time of those who are on staff.

I'm sure there are some great joys and rewards. Tell us your favorite.

I love to hear from students. Sharing in their successes as they graduate or move on in their careers is the greatest reward of teaching.

Did you start in another specialty?

Public sector paralegal representing clients in social security disability cases and assisting elderly clients with various elder law issues

We all hear how miserable the pay is for teachers. Does that apply to paralegal program instructors, professors, adjunct professors and directors?

By comparison to the pay of the average community college instructors, I am paid well. By comparison to the average earnings of paralegals in my geographic area and with similar experience I am paid well above the average.

Was it easy to find a job like this? How did you find this position?

I found the instructor position advertised in a local newspaper. I became the program coordinator/director about five years later by promotion.

There are many, many paralegals out there who would love to get out of the law firm and into something else without leaving the field. What advice would you give them?

For those seeking to get into my specialty I would advise them to pursue a higher degree, at least one level above the level at which they desire to teach. I would also suggest that they contact a paralegal program director and discuss the possibilities of working as an adjunct instructor.

Although it sounds like you are very busy, you must have time for fun.
I sing and travel with a gospel recording group called "PURPOSE".

Are you actively involved in any professional associations?
Oh, yes. I'm very involved as a North Carolina State Bar Certified Paralegal (NCCP), member of the North Carolina State Bar Board of Paralegal Certification's Paralegal Certification Committee (charged with the responsibility of creating the certification examination for State Bar certified paralegals), Institutional member of the American Association for Paralegal Educators, the North Carolina State Employees Association. I have published a number of CLE documents and presented at various national and statewide legal and educational conventions.

You've been here a long time and counseled many students. What's your future?
Consulting and training in the fields of continuing legal education and various aspects of leadership development.

Chapter Sixteen
Pharmaceutical, Biotech & Scientific Careers

Pharmaceutical companies are avid employers of paralegals in all types of specialties including corporate, litigation, corporate governance, trademark, patent, copyright and more. Working for a pharmaceutical company can involve protecting patents and trademarks; products liability; litigation; corporate transactional; and other practice specialties. A definite plus to getting hired in a pharmaceutical company are those with backgrounds in medical, biochemical or scientific arenas. Paralegals in these organizations or the law firms that represent them can be involved in massive and complex litigation cases, some of which hit the news and media on a regular basis.

Examples of Pharmaceutical Paralegal Positions

Sr. Paralegal
Research and Development

Provide prompt, accurate legal support and assistance to in-house counsel and client groups (including discovery research, alliances and partnerships, clinical, purchasing, regulatory, pharmaceutical sciences, and more. Negotiate, draft and review R&D agreements. Negotiate, draft and review HIPPA and informed consent documentation. Advise clients of internal (e.g. contract approval process) and legal requirements for R&D transactions. Conduct legal research. Participate in due diligence activities relating to R&D transactions. Keep apprised of issues relevant to pharmaceutical industry and accurately relay this information to clients. Work with client groups, third parties and outside counsel to identify, assess and address general legal concerns.

What You Need to Succeed: Bachelor's degree and formal legal training, or a Bachelor's degree in legal studies, or High School Diploma or AAS and equivalent legal training and/or work experience. Stable work background always. Experience performing substantive legal work, knowledge of the pharmaceutical industry a plus. Must be a team player, able to meet critical deadlines.

Where You Might Find This Position: Sanofi Aventis; Wyeth; Novartis; TAP; Bayer and many other organizations.

Stacey Hunt

Freelance Paralegal
San Luis Obispo, CA

Author, Writer, Paralegal Extraordinaire

Located right near the Pacific coast in a small, upscale California town not too far from the famous Hearst Castle, you'll find Stacey Hunt, a paralegal with a big heart, sharp mind and impressive paralegal leadership background.

Hunt, a paralegal crusader and co-author of the Business and Professions Code 6450, a bill that changed the way California Paralegals can enter and stay in the field, is a well-known advocate of the paralegal profession. Author of many books in the paralegal field, Hunt has managed to capture quite a bit of attention from paralegals, legislators, attorneys and associations through her writing, speaking and association activities. Past-President of the California Association for Paralegal Associations, and successful seminar leader, Hunt has safely secured a place in the annals of paralegal history.

Presently, she works as an independent paralegal for several law firms in the San Luis Obispo legal community. Here is what she has to say:

As an independent paralegal, where do you work?
I work for two sole practitioners, one 2-laywer firm, one 4-lawyer firm and a community services district (public agency).

What is your background?
I worked as a legal secretary for two years, went to school and got paralegal certificate, and have been a paralegal for the last 22 years.

Do you mind if I ask your age? (or decade)
I'll be 50 – tomorrow, as a matter of fact!

How long have you been in your present position?
I have been freelancing for 5 years now.

What motivated you to go out on your own?
I was unhappy and felt restricted working in law firms, but I still loved what I did. I thought I might get more challenge and variety by going out on my own.

What are the striking differences from working in a law firm to working on your own?
I love being able to set my own hours and come and go when I please. I love being able to work from home when I want. I love being in a different place every day, as I have a very low boredom threshold. On the downside, you feel less a part of the law firm "community", so you have to not mind feeling a bit of a loner. There are no paid holidays or vacations, no sick leave and no retirement, which presses you to work harder to make up for those things.

What are the similarities?
You still have to be mindful of your billable time - for you if not for an employer.

What are your assignments?
Legal and factual research, work with clients, review and organize documents, propound and answer discovery, attend depositions, hearings and trials, assist in coming up with case strategies.

You have quite an extensive writing career. You've written several books, you're a columnist for a popular paralegal magazine and 'your articles appear in many publications. Tell us more about your writing.
I was one of those weird kids in high school who actually *liked* researching and writing term papers! I love teaching people and I have found that gathering mounds of scattered information and turning it into a written piece that enlightens people or explains things to them in a new way they can understand is very satisfying. I will get an idea for an article when I am curious about something and satisfy my own curiosity by doing some research on it. Then I want to share it with others.

I started small by writing articles for my local paralegal association newsletter and worked my way up. I have now co-authored two general interest books for paralegals and one textbook. I have written numerous articles for *Legal Assistant Today* and have been a litigation and ethics columnist for the magazine. I have also written articles for *the Law Practice Management & Technology Section* and the *Public Law Section* of the California State Bar.

What motivated you to work on B&P 6450? How long did it take to get that through to passing? Was this your idea or yours and others? What was the purpose?

It had long been a dream of the CAPA board to have some sort of rules in place about who could use the title of "paralegal." We had all suffered the embarrassment of unqualified, untrained or uneducated people bestowing the title upon them and then performing poor quality work. Or worse yet, sullying the title by committing the unauthorized practice of law. I was personally motivated by a bad experience I had at a firm where a partner's daughter, who needed a job, was given the title paralegal, even though she knew nothing about the law. Suddenly this person was my peer and I had to train her! I knew some day I wanted to do something about it, and I was lucky enough to be in the right place at the right time on the CAPA board.

It took us many years to accomplish our goal. The board first tried to get some limited regulation through via the State Bar, but that fell through. We then went for a Supreme Court rule, but that failed as well. Introducing legislation was our third and ultimately successful attempt to establish a title that meant something. Now to call themselves paralegals, individuals must have earned a paralegal certificate, a BA or higher degree, must work with attorney supervision, and must complete continuing education.

How do you think it's been received in California? By employers? By paralegals?
At first there was a lot of resistance to any form of regulation. Even the CAPA board was not unanimous in getting the legislation through. However over time people have come to realize the value of what CAPA accomplished. The "fly-by-night" schools that promised a paralegal certificate in a few weekends have folded up. District attorneys have a new way of prosecuting people who call themselves paralegals but work directly with the public. Some employers do not insist on qualified people and do not insist their paralegals obtain their MCLE, but a recent federal case that was decided in California may change that. The case denied the recovery of paralegal fees to a firm whose paralegal was not in compliance with the code.

Do you think other states will follow? What further regulation do you think paralegals might need, if any?
Other states have already begun following the California scheme. Some already had some regulation in place even before California did. At this time, further

regulation would only limit, not expand what paralegals can do. I would love to see a time when paralegals could make appearances in court on uncontested matters or calendar calls.

Do you believe this change to the profession will increase salaries?
The legislation has been in place since 2001. Salaries have gone up, but I think it is a matter of across the board increases in the country, not necessarily just in California.

What advice would you give to paralegals that look to have a hand in changing the profession as you do?
You must have a great passion for this profession and get involved on a state and national level. Being surrounded by many other people who share your passion will spur you on take it to new heights.

What has been your toughest challenge?
Balancing too much work with too little work.

What has been your greatest reward?
Being my own boss.

How is the pay in that kind of position?
Very good. The challenge can be filling up the billable hours with work.

How do you find your jobs?
Mostly word-of-mouth from other people.

How many years of paralegal experience do you bring to the table?
Twenty-two years.

Did you start in another specialty?
After doing litigation for many years, I was hired by a city attorney and learned to do municipal law.

What do you do for fun?
I read, go wine tasting, and watch movies.

Do you participate in any professional activities?
I am the past-president of the California Association for Paralegal Associations (CAPA) and I am active in state and local paralegal associations.

What advice would you give other paralegals seeking freelance?
Paralegals who want to freelance should have a lot of experience (the law firms you work in will not want to train you - they expect you to hit the ground running), be well connected in the community, have a good office set up so that

you don't have to depend on equipment provided by clients, and be prepared to work hard.

What's your next step?
I am happy doing what I am doing right now for the present.

Anything you'd like to add?
By choosing a specialty wisely, a freelancer can leverage his or her value to clients. Litigation paralegals are a dime a dozen, so we don't command the highest rates. My friends who do probate, corporate and Medi-Cal work can charge double what I do.

Hot Tip

If you are seeking more money and can't find a survey that gives you the information you need, try calling your local headhunters or legal staffing organizations.

They have the "inside" information and usually a more updated handle on the current market in your region. You don't have to be seeking a new position for them to assist you. Recruiters are usually happy to make new contacts and welcome the call.

Be sure you contact an agency that handles legal staffing. They are "in the know".

Chapter Seventeen
The All New Legal Assistant Today
Salary Survey
(Reprinted with permission)

Looking back on the paralegal profession and salary compensation is like going back to your high school reunion. At a reunion, you can see who has changed the most, who has stayed the same and who is the most successful. At *Legal Assistant Today*, we are celebrating a reunion of sorts with our annual salary survey. Since 1991, *LAT* has published results from 15 salary surveys (surveys were not published in 1994 and 1995). To mark this milestone, we glance back at the profession and paralegal compensation 15 years ago, plus provide you with up-to-date salary and benefits information from our latest survey.

Reflection

In 1990, when *LAT* first surveyed its readers (see the survey results in May/June 1991 *LAT*), legal assistants across the country were making an average salary of $27,772, while paralegals with more than 10 years of experience were making an average of $32,107. Flash forward to the 2006 survey results: The average salary was $51,771, about 86 percent more than in

1990.

The current survey also found paralegals with 10 to 15 years of experience averaged $50,651 (17.8 percent of respondents), and those with 15 to 20 years of experience averaged $60,664 (20 percent of respondents).

Toby Marchionno-Adams, a litigation and intellectual property paralegal for Meyer, Unkovic & Scott in Pittsburgh, started out in the legal community as an intern, then she was a secretary, and now she has been a paralegal for more than 10 years. Throughout the years, Marchionno-Adams has worked in a solo practitioner's office, a small firm with fewer than 10 attorneys, and a medium-sized firm with about 60 attorneys. During this time, she has seen a trend when comparing salary and firm size. "Salary compensation seems to go hand in hand with the size of the firm," she said. "The larger the firm, the higher the salary."

In Columbia, S.C., Vicki Lynn Mitchell, a 15-year paralegal specializing in litigation, intellectual property and administrative law for Neasden Prêt, said She has seen many changes in the legal landscape. "The fact that so many firms now classify paralegals as nonexempt has been a major change," she said. "This occurred at my firm several years ago. At first I was not happy with the change. I have since changed my mind because I think it helped my employer recognize the level of effort the paralegals at my firm put into their careers every day."

According to *LAT*'s survey results, 57 percent of respondents said they are nonexempt. Another change Mitchell has seen in South Carolina is that many firms are instituting merit bonuses in addition to paying overtime. "Prior to 2006, my employer awarded bonuses based on seniority. In 2006, a new bonus system was instituted that is based on billable hours and collections," she said. "This new system gives the paralegals an opportunity to increase their income."

One of the most dramatic changes over the years has been in technology. In 1990, the most sought-after technology skills that survey respondents mentioned were computer literacy, word processing and data entry.

Today, advanced computer skills and the ability to use all kinds of software are requirements of the job, and Mitchell said she has definitely noticed the change. "I use litigation support software everyday," she said. "When I first started working as a paralegal, e-mail was new and everyone had a calendar with deadlines on their desks."

Salary Survey Results

Highest Full-Time Salary
$110,000

Lowest Full-Time Salary
$23,000

Average Salary
$51,771
Up 1.4% from 2005

Average Salary by Employer
Law Firm $50,666
Corporate $59,453
Government $55,719

Highest Raise
$13,000

Average Raise
$3,456 - $1,012 more than the average raise in 2005.
74.6%   Received Raise

Highest Bonus
$24,000

Average Bonus
$2,962
66.1% Received Bonus

Average Bonus by Employer
Law Firm $3,208
Corporate $4,354
Government $505

Paralegal Positions
Increased   21.0%
Stayed the Same   64.8%
Decreased   14.2%

National and Regional Salary Pulse

Average paralegal salaries might have gone up more than $23,000 since 1990, but salaries only went up 1.4 percent from 2005 to 2006, and many paralegals aren't satisfied with their pay. While more than 63 percent of respondents said they are paid fairly, this figure is almost 10 percent less than just one year ago.

"I feel unfairly compensated because I did take the time to go back to school, which helped increase my worth and moved my career to a higher level," said Tara David, a 4-year corporate legal assistant who specializes in contracts in the entertainment industry in Universal City, Calif. "There are other paralegals in my area making more than I do, but they are not functioning as paralegals. They are functioning at various levels of management titles. The paralegals that are functioning as paralegals are not happy with their compensation."

Paralegals in the corporate sector came out on top of the salary compensation race, with the average corporate paralegal making $59,453. The top five paying corporate specialties were: ethics ($86,000), mergers and acquisitions ($65,963), securities ($65,958), contracts ($60,833) and intellectual property ($60,646).

Paralegals in the law firm setting made an average salary of $50,666 in 2006, with the highest paying specialties including: securities ($69,600), intellectual property ($58,853), product liability ($53,875), civil rights ($51,500) and litigation ($51,495).

In 1990, the highest-paid specialties were corporate law, labor and employment, consumer law and environmental. In 2006, several of those specialties are still in the highest-paid category. "Corporate, labor and employment (ERISA), trusts and estates, and intellectual property — specifically foreign trademark filing — have been the highest in paralegal compensation and the most often requested paralegal specialty areas from our clients, both law firms and corporations," Grandzol said. "The apparent shortage of supply and increase in demand for experienced paralegals having this type of knowledge has led to a dramatic increase in compensation within these practice areas."

Every region in the United States saw an increase in paralegal salaries except the Southern region. The Northeast region saw the most dramatic increase with an average paralegal salary of $59,729, up 13.6 percent from the previous year. Midwest region salaries increased 1.8 percent for an average salary of $47,814, and Western region salaries increased 1.7 percent for an average salary of $55,882. Salaries in the southern part of the United States decreased by 3.7 percent with an average salary of $48,014.

Raises, Bonuses and Benefits

Although paralegals didn't see a huge jump in their salaries in 2006, 69.5 percent received a bonus with the average bonus being $3,107.

Average Salary by Years of Experience

Years of Experience	Average Salary	Percentage of Respondents
More than 20	$56,222	21.7%
15 to 20	$60,664	20.0%
10 to 15	$50,651	10.4%
7 to 10	$49,667	10.4%
5 to 7	$46,676	7.8%
3 to 5	$41,897	6.3%
1 to 3	$37,843	10.4%
Less than 1 year	$44,250	3.5%

Average Salary by Specialty for Those Working in a Law Firm Setting

Specialty	Average Salary	Percentage of Respondents
Administrative	$41,2546	5.3%
Bankruptcy	$42,395	7.7%
Business	$43,818	10.1%
Civil Rights	$51,500	4.1%
Commercial	$47,582	7.1%
Contracts	$42,591	8.9%
Corporation & Enterprise	$47,360	15.4%
Criminal	$41,380	8.3%
Environmental	$38,500	2.4%
Family	$38,772	16.0%
Injury & Tort	$42.830	14.2%
Insurance	$43,752	5.3%
Intellectual Property	$58,853	5.3%
Labor & Employment	$47,663	8.9%
Litigation	$51,495	46.7%
Medical Malpractice	$44,650	14.8%
Personal Injury – Defense	$43,744	9.5%
Personal Injury – Plaintiff	$41,074	23.1%
Probate, Trusts & Estates	$46,735	21.3%

Product Liability	$53,875	4.7%
Securities	$69,600	3.0%
Tax	$40,228	3.6%
Workers' Compensation	$37,791	10.1%

Average Salary by Specialty for Those Working in a Corporate Legal Setting

Specialty	Average Salary	Percentage of Respondents
Asset-based Lending	$32,000	5.9%
Contracts	$60,833	39.2%
Corporate Governance	$60,833	37.3%
Ethics	$86,000	5.9%
Intellectual Property	$60,646	19.6%
International	$57,124	9.8%
Labor	$56,667	19.6%
Litigation	$51,364	45.1%
Mergers & Acquisitions	$65,963	23.5%
Real Estate	$42,035	17.6%
Securities	$65,958	17.6%

William Hershkowitz, a 14-year paralegal working in a small general practice law firm in New York City, said since he has worked in the field, he has received adequate raises and bonuses every year. "I believe my firm recognizes the importance of bonuses and raises," he said.

Marchionno-Adams echoed that sentiment. She has received a raise each year she has worked at her current firm, but she said bonuses aren't always expected. "[Raises] show employees their work is noticed and appreciated," she said.

One thing that hasn't changed much in 15 years: When it comes to compensation, money isn't everything. In 1990, many survey respondents commented on the value that benefits added to their compensation package, with the top perks including health insurance (79.6 percent), life insurance (76.6 percent) and a company-sponsored retirement plan (70.2 percent).

According to our 2006 survey, benefits are still vital today, with many respondents receiving paid vacation (85.2 percent), health benefits (81 percent), life insurance (62 percent) and dental insurance (61.2 percent). Other less common but noteworthy benefits received in 2006 include: The employer paying for association memberships (59.1 percent), allowing flexible schedules

(38 percent), providing work-from-home opportunities (17.3 percent) and paying for a cell phone (9.7 percent).

Gerard Grandzol, placement director for Special Counsel in Philadelphia, has seen this change in technology increase the demand for skilled, trained paralegals. "Over the past 15 years, legal recruiters have had an emphatic impact on paralegal movement within the industry," he said. "Law firms and corporate counsels now have established placement fees and retained search budgets as paralegal positions become more technical and as experienced paralegals are in higher demand."

Grandzol said most law firms and corporations today offer paralegal employees health, vision, dental, short and long-term disability and retirement plans. "Many actually offer pension plans in addition to 401(k) s, health and wellness plans, flex-spending accounts, flex-time schedules and profit sharing, on-site fitness centers and on-site child care facilities," he said. "Benefits do take the place of more salary, especially as health care and insurance costs have dramatically risen over the past several years."

While Hershkowitz's firm pays the lion's share of medical and drug coverage, he said there are other perks that come with working for a small firm. For example, he isn't micromanaged and is able to set his own schedule. "My attorneys will give me a project and basically tell me we need to get from point A to point E and leave it to me to research and get it done," he said. "This is the most rewarding work, as it's creative and intellectually stimulating."

Great benefits are extremely important to David, who has a daughter. "The most rewarding benefits to me are the medical, dental, vision and flexibility," she said. "I feel confident in being covered for preventive medical issues, and when there are school meetings, basketball games and no school days, I can work out a flexible schedule with my boss."

Average Salary by Firm Size

Number of Attorneys	Average Salary
101 plus	$67,471
51 to 100	$59,978
26 to 50	$56,015
11 to 25	$52,024
6 to 10	$52,159
2 to 5	$45,356
0 to 1	$45,812

The Education Factor

Fifteen years ago, the average salary for a paralegal with a bachelor's degree was $28,644, more than $800 above the national average. Today, education is an even larger determining factor when an employer is hiring a paralegal. More than 47 percent of respondents said they have a bachelor's degree (with an average salary of $54,268, which is well over the national average). The 6.9 percent of respondents who have a master's degree averaged $61,655 last year.

How are bonus amounts determined?
(Respondents selected all that applied)

Total number of billable hours	9.6%
Market	10.7%
Years of service	13.5%
Firm percentage of salary	19.7%
Firm success	21.9%
Supervisor or attorney discretion	52.8%

How long ago was your most recent salary review? at your current place of employment?

3 months or less	14.5%
4 to 6 months	19.1%
7 months to 1 year	31.1%
More than 1 year	16.6%
No review with this employer	18.7%

What is the average number of hours you work per week?

Less than 10	3.0%
11 to 25	2.6%
26 to 37	5.1%
38 to 40	39.7%
41 to 50	47.4%
51 or more	2.1%

Average Hourly Billing Rate

Billing Rate	Percentage Responding
$156 or more	9.0%
$136 to $155	9.0%
$96 to $115	12.4%
$86 to $95	21.3%
$76 to $85	9.0%
$66 to $75	12.4%
$56 to $65	6.7%
$46 to $55	1.1%
$26 to $35	2.2%
$15 to $25	2.2%

What was the minimum number of billable hours you were required to meet for 2006?

Number of Hours Required	Percentage Responding
More than 2,000	1.8%
1,801 to 2,000	1.8%
1,601 to 1,800	10.9%
1,401 to 1,600	20.0%
1,001 to 1,200	2.7%
801 to 1,000	1.8%
601 to 800	3.6%
400 to 600	0.9%
No minimum identified	50%

What types of duties do you find yourself doing most often at work? (Respondents selected all that applied)

Type of Duty	Percentage Responding
Clerical	38.8%
Client relations	53.4%
Document management	76.7%
Drafting documents	73.7%
Project management	39.2%
Research	44.0%
Secretarial	33.2%
Trial preparation	31.5%

What percentage of your time is spent on non-billable tasks?

0% to 5%	9.5%
6% to 10%	19.0%
11% to 20%	19.0%
21% to 30%	13.8%
31% to 40%	12.1%
41% to 50%	12.1%
More than 50%	14.7%

Exempt vs. Nonexempt

	Avg. Salary
Exempt 43.0%	$52,704
Nonexempt 57.0%	$50,523

Years of Experience

	Law Firm	Corporate	Government
Less than 3	80.0%	16.0%	4.0%
3 to 5	66.7%	13.3%	20.0%
5 to 7	64.3%	14.3%	21.4%
7 to 10	78.9%	5.3%	15.8%
10 to 15	70.3%	0.0%	29.7%

15 to 20	62.5%	7.5%	30.0%
More than 20	73.3%	11.1%	15.6%

Bonus and Raise Amounts

	Law Firm	Corporate	Government
Average Bonus	$3,224	$4,354	$505
Received Bonus	79.3%	57.5%	29.4%
Raise Amount	$3,282	$3,575	$4,220

Paralegal Positions at Firm/Department

	Law Firm	Corporate	Government
Increased	19.4%	28.9%	18.8%
Stayed the Same	64.9%	60.6%	62.4%
Decreased	15.7%	10.5%	18.8%

Do you think you are paid fairly?

Respondents who said yes.

Law Firm	64.5%
Corporate	75.0%
Government	58.8%

What is your official job title?

Title	Percentage Responding
Educator	.05%
Lawyer's assistant	0.0%
Legal assistant	16.8%
Legal document assistant	0.0%
Student	0.5%
Legal secretary	2.6%
Paralegal	58.2%
Paralegal/legal assistant manager	5.1%
Senior paralegal/legal assistant	16.3%

How many paralegals and attorneys are in your firm or department?

Number of Paralegals	Percentage Responding	Number of Attorneys	Percentage Responding
101 plus	2.6%	101 plus	8.1%
51 to 100	3.0%	51 to 100	6.8%
26 to 50	3.8%	26 to 50	11.5%
11 to 25	9.4%	11 to 25	17.9%
6 to 10	12.8%	6 to 10	10.3%
2 to 5	38.3%	2 to 5	33.3%
0 to 1	30.2%	0 to 1	12.0%

How many paralegals are in your firm or department?

Number of Attorneys

0 to 1	12.0%	$45,812
2 to 5	33.3%	$45,356
6 to 10	10.3%	$52,159
11 to 25	17.9%	$52,024
26 to 50	11.5%	$56,015
51 to 100	6.8%	$59,978
101 plus	8.1%	$67,471

Average Paralegal Salary in Firms with This Number of Paralegals

0 to 1	30.2%	$45,812
2 to 5	38.3%	$50,588
6 to 10	12.8%	$53,229
11 to 25	9.4%	$61,313
26 to 50	3.8%	$54,350
51 to 100	3.0%	$65,512
101 plus	2.6%	$67,583

What kind of staffing support do you receive in your work environment? (Respondents selected all that applied)

Share a secretary	34.6%

A file clerk	22.8%
Word processing	12.2%
A secretary	6.8%
A receptionist	35.0%
A project assistant	10.1%

Does your employer provide formal, in-house paralegal training?

No	85.6%
Yes	14.4%

Did you work in a different profession before becoming a paralegal?

Yes	72.9%
No	27.1%

In the past 12 months, have you looked for a new job within the paralegal profession?

Yes	14.9%
No	57.0%
Undecided	28.1%

In the next 12 months, do you plan to look for a new job within the paralegal profession?

Yes	7.5%
No	76.2%
Undecided	16.3%

How did you obtain your present job?
(Respondents selected all that applied)

Internet	10.2%
Internship	4.2%
Moved with attorney	6.5%

Networking/friend	32.9%
Newspaper	17.6%
Placement agency	13.4%
Promotion	5.6%
School placement office	3.7%
Unsolicited résumé	10.6%

In the past 12 months, have you been laid-off or downsized?

Yes	53.6%
No	46.4%

If yes, were you successful in finding a new job within the paralegal profession? If yes, how long did your search take?

Less than 1 month	37.8%
1 to 3 months	29.7%
4 to 6 months	13.5%
7 to 9 months	8.1%
10 to 12 months	2.7%
More than 1 year	8.1%

For hiring purposes, what minimum requirement does your current employer have for paralegals?

Certificate from an ABA-approved paralegal program	41.1%
Certificate from a non-ABA-approved paralegal program	9.4%
Associate of arts/science degree	14.6%
Bachelor of arts/science degree	26.6%
Paralegal experience	49.5%
Professional designation	2.6%
No educational requirement	16.1%
No paralegal experience requirement	15.6%

What is the highest level of formal, general education you have completed?

	Percentage	Avg. Salary

High school	2.6%	$47,180
Some college	17.7%	$45,445
Associate's degree	24.1%	$48,900
Bachelor's degree	47.4%	$54,268
Master's degree	6.9%	$61,655
Doctorate	1.3%	$55,734

Average Salary by Certificate

Association	Percentage	Salary
American Alliance Certified Paralegal (AACP)	0.4%	$52,000
NALA's Advanced Certified Paralegal	1.7%	$44,800
NALA's Certified Legal Assistant (CLA)	14.8%	$57,149
NALA's Certified Paralegal (CP)	8.4%	$47,689
NALA's Certified Legal Assistant Specialist (CLAS)	3.0%	$58,271
NALS' Certified Professional Paralegal (Certified PP)	2.1%	$40,333
NFPA's Registered Paralegal (RP)	5.5%	$59,289
State Certification	4.2%	$55,929

West Region

Average Salary $55,882   Up 1.7% from 2005

Average Raises and Bonuses

Average Raise	$3,429	Received Raise	69.4%
Average Bonus Amount	$2,985	Received Bonus	64.6%

Average Salary By Employer

Law Firm	$52,119	71.4%
Corporate	$56,043	19.0%
Government	$90,652	9.5%

Average Bonus by Employer

Law Firm	$3,371
Corporate	$1,495
Government	N/A

Paralegal Positions at Work

Increased	11.4%
Stayed the Same	79.5%
Decreased	9.1%

Midwest Region

Average Salary $47,814   Up 1.8% from 2005

Average Salary by Employer

Law Firm	$48,305	70.6%
Corporate	$48,102	17.6%
Government	$41,785	11.8%

Raises and Bonuses

Average Raise	$3,230	Received Raise	82.8%
Average Bonus Amount	$3,048	Received Bonus	69.4%

Average Bonus by Employer

Law Firm	$3,294
Corporate	$3,027
Government	$ 75

Paralegal Positions at Work

Increased	13.3%
Stayed the Same	71.7%
Decreased	15.0%

Northeast Region

Average Salary $59,729   Up 13.6& from 2005

Average Salary by Employer

Law Firm	$60,709	84.4%
Corporate	$71,690	15.6%
Government	N/A	0.0%

Raises and Bonuses

Average Raise	$3,638	Received Raise	70.3%
Average Bonus Amount	$3,312 +	Received Bonus	75.7%

Average Bonus by Employer

Law Firm	$3,383
Corporate	$5,400
Government	N/A

Paralegal Positions at Work

Increased	25.7%
Stayed the Same	62.9%
Decreased	11.4%

South Region

Average Salary $48,014   Down 3.7% from 2005

Average Salary by Employer

Law Firm	$45,212	65.8%
Corporate	$61,506	24.7%
Government	$42,898	9.6%

Average Bonus by Employer

Law Firm	$2,950
Corporate	$4,883
Government	$ 613

Paralegal Positions at Work

Increased	30.4%
Stayed the Same	51.9%
Decreased	17.7%

Methodology

LAT conducted its 2006 salary survey by mailing questionnaires to a random sampling of 2,000 of *LAT*'s current, paid subscribers. The resulting data is illustrated in the included charts and includes a margin of error of plus or minus 6.33 percent. Final data was compiled from the 11.85 percent of respondents who completed the survey and returned it by the Dec. 8, 2006 deadline.

Office of the State Appellate Defender
Belleville, IL

Paralegal Profile: MaryAnn Campbell
Death Penalty Paralegal

Where do you work?
I work for the Office of the State Appellate Defender, Death Penalty Trial Assistance Office, Belleville, IL. We have 2 other offices, one in Springfield, IL and one in Chicago, IL

What is your background?
Over the years, I have worked as a soda fountain clerk, (A LONG TIME AGO!), inventory clerk, title corrections clerk for the State of Missouri and also for the State of Missouri, in the Delinquent Tax Division.

I have worked as Human Resources clerk, data entry clerk, then a school secretary before I decided that I needed a career that would utilize the skills I had, so I began to explore the paralegal field. I enrolled at Southwestern Illinois College in Belleville, IL, in the paralegal program that they had.   I worked for 4 years at the firm of Amelung, Wulff & Willenbrock in St. Louis, MO, as the paralegal for the medical malpractice team of Mr. Robert A. Wulff, and associates.

Do you mind if I ask your age?
Fifty-one.

How long have you been in your present position?
Three and one-half years.

How many years of experience do you have?
Eight years

Tell me about the nature of your assignments.
Our office assists attorneys who have indigent clients charged with capital crimes. In Illinois, in Death Penalty Cases, 2 attorneys have to be appointed or hired, who are certified by the Capital Litigation Trial Bar. Once these attorneys are appointed then they can ask or we can offer our help.

When we get a case, I go through the discovery to determine if we have the crime scene photos and the autopsy report. I organize it, and prepare a brief summary of the discovery. (This is my goal for every case, but I don't always get it all done). If the staff attorney has some area of law that he needs research done, I may help out there as well. I assist the defense team in any way that I can. I prepare our staff investigator's notebooks. He gets a copy o the discovery and I often assist him in breaking it down in the format he likes, so he can develop leads on witnesses.

I have tracked down witnesses, interviewed witnesses, gone with our Forensic Social Historian on visits. I sometimes attend motion hearings just to see what is going on with our case. I try to keep the docket sheets current in our files.

I may be asked to burn/copy discovery when it comes in on DVD's or CD Roms. I locate experts and set up meetings with the defense team with that expert, if asked to do so. I worked on a major homicide case out of Cook County with a crime scene Reconstructionist and his staff to get (try to) 300,000 pages of discovery in some kind of order. We worked together to go through the material to prepare reports for the lead attorneys and the judge on the case in Cook County. We prepared a Power Point presentation of the material to several people involved in this case.

I draft routine correspondence to clients or court clerks regarding the cases. I have gone with the staff attorney to a crime scene. I built a Lego "crime scene" with some help, on a large case in Cook County. I also work with Southwestern Illinois College's intern program for paralegals. We get one or two of them a year. I work with the staff attorney to train them to go out and be paralegals. They already have the "book learning" as some would say, and we try to help them put the theories into practice.

What has been your toughest challenge?

To not let the awful things I see or hear, prevent me from assisting our clients with their defense. It would be easy to do what everyone else does and just toss them away, to take the back seat. We are "BEHIND the SCENES" and often have to wait on the lead attorney. I was used to picking up the phone and getting the information I need right away. Patience is not one of my virtues.

What was your greatest reward?

To know that while I may not change the world's outlook on the death penalty, I can change it one person at a time where I am at.

How is the pay in that kind of position?

I believe that the salary I receive is very fair.

How did you find your job?

I was looking for a job outside of the law firm arena. A friend of mine called to tell me about an advertisement in the St Louis Dispatch. I sent in my resume and interviewed. It was a new position that had just been created for the agency.

Did you start out in another specialty?

Yes. I was a civil litigation paralegal first at an insurance defense firm.

What advice would you give other paralegals seeking to get into your specialty?

You have to pay your dues first. So work hard, and get some experience, and then go for the gold. Always be willing to learn something new.

I am not a "techie". But our agency needed some research done on discovery management software and trial software. I volunteered. Then went "OOPS!" But it was a very good assignment and helped me understand what is out there to help me do my job better. Listen and ask questions. Volunteer for that extra project. Trust your judgment. Even if you make a mistake, the beauty of the law, (as I was told as a newbie) is that most everything can be corrected.

Chapter Eighteen

Real Estate
Big Deals = Bigger Opportunities

There might not be another position besides the corporate transactional job that is so tightly tied to the ups-and-downs of the economy the real estate market. When the market is up, real estate paralegals are in demand. Down goes the market, away go the relatively high-paying and highly developed positions. In a hot market, there are lists and lists of real estate positions, almost all of them wanting you to start immediately.

Despite its vulnerability, real estate is appealing to many paralegals. You might find yourself drafting complicated leasing agreements, working with the Department of Real Estate, high-end developers, tract housing, shopping malls, participate in closings, or work with titles, surveys, deeds of trust and other instruments. Here's a very exciting specialty in which it would probably behoove you to get cross-training in other paralegal arenas.

Real Estate Paralegal; Mergers & Acquisitions, Closings

As a Real Estate paralegal, there are opportunities to work in law firms, corporate legal departments, government agencies, non-profit organizations, solo practitioners, real estate development companies, title companies with attorneys and clients in real estate transactions from buying and selling properties, title review, closings, mergers & acquisitions, Department of Real Estate, and more.

Commercial Transactional and Leasing Real Estate Paralegal

Preparation, drafting and reviewing of leases and other collateral documents; review exceptions to titles & prepare necessary documents to correct or clear title; order/review survey and prepare legal description; work with Commercial Real Estate Finance.

Salaries: Atlanta – 5-7 years: $55-68,000 per year.

Real Estate Paralegal – Acquisitions, Sales & Loans

Ability to coordinate acquisitions and sales and loan transactions; review title and survey; draft closing documentation; prepare complex adjustment statements; organize and attend closings.

What You Need to Succeed: BA/BS Degree Paralegal certificate from ABA Approved program; Mid-large law firm experience; 5-10 years experience as a Real Estate paralegal

Salaries: $75-85,000 (in Los Angeles).

Leasing Coordinator for Broadcast Station & Law Firms

Leasing Coordinator to take ownership of projects, assisting in securing lease sites, monitoring the progress of equipment installation and station builds, and do lease negotiations. Deal with landlords, outside vendors, engineers, project managers, attorneys, etc. Although a legal, lease/real estate or engineering background would be helpful, analytical skills, attention to detail, organizational skills and excellent communication skills are absolutely required.

Where You Might Find This Position: EMF Broadcasting, parent ministry of K-LOVE & Air 1 Christian radio networks. Also check restaurant chains; real estate law firms; mall developers; banks, real estate developers; law firms and in-house legal departments.

Real Estate Paralegal in Housing & Development Company

Assist the Vice President and Development Director in underwriting affordable housing acquisitions, assemblage and review of due diligence materials for new acquisitions, assist in assembling financing applications, and assist in real estate and loan closings.

What You Need to Succeed: At least 5 years of experience in commercial real estate and commercial loan transactions including title and survey work. Strong communication skills, able to work with others, accountable for adherence to deadlines and timetables, and be detail oriented.

Real Estate Paralegal – Triple Net Properties Real Estate

Provide support for all aspects of Triple Net Properties real estate transactions including acquisitions, dispositions, and financing. Negotiate and close a wide variety of real estate transactions. Involved with leasing, property due diligence, property management and general dispute resolution.

Acquisitions/Dispositions:

- Assist Real Estate Counsel in negotiating purchase and sale contracts and structuring and closing transactions.
- Oversee coordination between acquisition underwriting and deal documents.
- Assist with property due diligence.
- Track deal progress and deliveries.
- Review major property documents.

Financing:

- Review loan documents and coordinate internal comments.
- Communicate with lenders and counsel regarding loan documents and deliveries.
- Track financing transactions and lender form documents.

What You Need to Succeed:

- Experience as a real estate paralegal at a major law firm. Bachelor's degree and paralegal certification (or equivalent)
- Experience in closing significant purchase and sale financing transactions, performing property due diligence and lease reviews, communicating with outside counsel and lenders, and drafting legal documents.

Real Estate Paralegal – Mountains of Western North Carolina

Experience in title research; examination of public records in Jackson, Macon and Transylvania counties. This firm advertised the benefits of working in a friendly, non-smoking office located in a historic, serene setting. Assistance with relocation and housing is available. Here's a great opportunity for professional growth and personal enrichment.

Salary: $25,000 - $30,000.

Hot Tip

When sending an e-mail to prospective employers, do not try to look "cool" by typing your e-mail in all lower case.

Many employers will not get a favorable impression!

Chapter Nineteen

Trusts & Estate Planning and Probate
For the Baby Boomer Crowd

You're going to need excellent accounting skills if you'd like to tackle a Trusts & Estate Planning positions. Tax preparation background is also helpful. Many T&E paralegals do have an opportunity to work directly with clients. Probate paralegals also must have excellent accounting and organizational skills and plenty of empathy to work with beneficiaries.

Trusts & Estate Planning and Probate paralegals are generally found in Mid-Size or smaller law firms, with solo practitioners or non-profit organizations. They tend to stay long-term and do not appear to bounce around in their careers. These paralegals take plenty of seminars in order to stay current with changing laws and overall, seem to have plenty of job satisfaction.

Examples of Trusts & Estate Planning Paralegal Positions

Trusts & Estate Planning Paralegal
Non-Profit Organization

Non-profits organizations see plenty of donations and gifts to the organization. Paralegals are responsible for the management and oversight of trust and estate administration for a non-profit organization bequest program. Maintain accurate bequest and financial information communicating with personal representatives and attorneys on estate and probate matters.

Assist with analysis of estate and trust litigation; perform in-depth analysis and audit of estate files and work with professional associates to resolve outstanding issues; perform annual review of estate files for closure; serve as a resource to the Gift Services Department staff and field personnel in resolving complex probate estate administration issues; perform highly specialized and technical activities.

What You Need to Succeed: Paralegal certificate from an accredited paralegal school or college degree, preferably in Public Administration, Business Administration or related field. Experience in probate/trust administration or tax/accounting background. In-depth knowledge of trust, estate and probate administration; investment vehicles, accounting methods and procedures; Probate Code; Revised Uniform Principal and Income Act as it pertains to investment of trust assets.

Where You Might Find This Position: Non-profit organizations such as Make-A-Wish Foundation and The Salvation Army; almost any large, charitable organizations.

Trusts & Estates/Probate Paralegal – Working with Beneficiaries

Gather estate asset and fiduciary information. Work directly with beneficiaries, file documents with the court, and prepare all estate and trust filings, including 706 returns. Ability to work independently is expected in these positions.

Probate Examiner
Superior Court of Orange County, CA

The Superior Court in Orange County, CA sought a Probate Examiner. Here's an opportunity for those who are wish to enter the probate specialty or for those who desire a change. Examine petitions, accountings, or other filed material relating to wills, conservatorships and other probate matters. Research While the position called for a law degree, it also required experience as a probate secretary and as a probate paralegal. Bilingual in Spanish/English language required.

Project Assistant – Document Management & Public Records

Organize and prepare documents for research public records using public websites, prepare forms, charts, letters, binders, copies. Enter data, and maintain files. Perform database research and data entry; obtain documents and other information from cities, municipalities or public agencies.

Assist paralegals and attorneys with mailings and filings; interact with clients; assist with estate planning and trust administration; draft general correspondence. Maintain case files; prepare documents for production and closing books. Gather cases and exhibit from files for incorporation into briefs.

What You Need to Succeed: Undergraduate degree and/or a paralegal certificate. 2-4 years' office experience preferably in a law firm environment supporting paralegals and/or attorneys. Word, Excel and Outlook. Prior estate planning and trust administration, account experience is helpful.

Tax, Trusts & Estates Paralegal – High-Income Clients

Generally dealing with high-income clients, large firm paralegals work with all aspects of the administration of estates, take instructions from clients, assess the value of estates, determine if inheritance tax is to be paid, prepare oaths apply and register the probate. Prepare non-tax planning wills, preparation and registration of Enduring Powers of Attorney/Lasting Powers of Attorney.

Chapter Twenty

The Demand for Technology and Litigation Support

Paralegals are excellent candidates for litigation support specialist because of their knowledge of courtroom and discovery procedures, pre-trial preparation, document management and local rules. A person with a solid litigation background plus expert knowledge of software can assist in the review, production and presentation of evidence. They may also be present at trial.

There's a lot of pressure to keep up in litigation support. Fewer skills in the legal field go out of date as quickly as technology and the need to keep current is critical. There's also the right fit for the job. Just because a paralegal possesses the abilities to perform the technical aspects of litigation support does not mean they can do the job. It takes a special blend of legal and technical knowledge combined the ability to impart the information, understand the urgency, legal system, and team dynamics along with the direct costs involved.

Skills involved besides expert knowledge of software include excellent teamwork talent, multi-tasking aptitude, problem solving, superior organizational ability, capability to work under tight deadlines and extreme pressure and a knack to process documents and evidence quickly.

E-discovery has created an entire new industry as more evidentiary issues involve e-mails, hard drives, voicemail and other electronic storage media. Additionally, the new Federal Rules that came about at the end of 2006 has pushed many changes into the forefront making it clear that paralegals need to get as involved as possible in the process.

Examples of Litigation Support Positions

Litigation Paralegal – Discovery Specialist, Document Management

Manage litigation, coordinate response to subpoenas and coordinate document review and productions. Coordinate case management; assist in document review and collection; coordinate and manage discovery process; conduct legal research; index and summarize transcripts and exhibits; organize and maintain document form files and client files; prepare legal documents for review, approval and use by attorneys. Coordinate and manage document production from receipt of subpoena to final production; institute and draft preservation notices; work closely with e-discovery vendors to process electronic data; document review and cataloguing; track subpoenas and status. Assist in the development of legal presentations; assist in maintaining matter tracking software.

What You Need to Succeed: Thorough knowledge of litigation. An advanced understanding of the technology supporting litigation efforts required. Knowledge in legal terminology required. Excellent computer skills with a high degree of accuracy for typical modern office computer software programs such as Microsoft Word, Excel, PowerPoint, online matter management database, other file databases, Westlaw, Lexis, Concordance, Opticon, and Adobe Acrobat. Ability to perform legal research using Westlaw or Lexis, Pacer, or other news or legal resources with minimal supervision or guidance required.

Education:

Bachelor's degree and/or paralegal certificate; plenty of continuing legal education for latest updates.

Salary: $35,000 - $75,000; paid overtime; bonus; vacation; full-benefits.

Litigation Support Analyst – Document Management

Supports attorneys and legal professionals in using litigation support tools in delivering client services; and in the use of litigation support tools for the preparation of cases and for trial.

Create and support document databases/indexes, transcripts, and images in Concordance, Summation, LiveNote, Microsoft Access, and like litigation support applications. Coordinate the project set up, scanning, coding, and OC ring of documents with outside vendors. Assist attorneys in preparing to use courtroom presentation tools; Setup and operation of these tools in the courtroom.

Maintain preferred vendor listing of equipment rental and litigation support service vendors. Possible certification required in one of the primary litigation support databases (Summation, Concordance). Serve as the point person in resolving software/hardware issues relating to the supported litigation support tools. Provide training in classroom settings, with litigation teams and one-on-one, in the use of litigation support tools. Provide summaries of each case to attorneys.

What You Need to Succeed: Concordance, LiveNote, Summation, Real Legal Binder, Microsoft Access, FolioViews, Adobe Acrobat and Doculex (or other similar viewer), Trial Director, Sanction, JFS Litigators Notebook. Experience with courtroom presentation tools. Working knowledge of personal computers and the Microsoft Office suite. Familiarity with Citrix and network operating systems.

Should have a college degree in relevant field or system-related technical certification. 1-2 years' experience as a litigation paralegal preferred.

Other Titles: Practice Support Analyst, Practice Support Coordinator; Sr. Litigation Support Analyst.

Salary: $75-95,000 plus OT (Boston); to $120,000 (in New York) plus bonus.

Where You Might Find This Position: Major, Mid-Sized law firms; in-house legal departments; government agencies and vendors.

Litigation Support Manager – Operations & Technology

The Litigation Support Manager is in charge of administrative, technical and operational integration for litigation support of attorneys, paralegal and support staff.

Work with internal clients to define requirements and management of evidence and case-related documents; provide on-going training; develop recommendations, case plans, cost-estimates, budgets, reference guides and procedures related to database configuration; trouble-shoot software configurations. Provide project management including selection of vendors; design and implementation of reports; review and load information into litigation databases. Manage team of litigation support staff and coders.

In-depth knowledge of electronic discovery and new amendments to the FRCP (Federal Rules of Civil Procedures). This includes searching and quality control auditing of databases and imagebases, printing reports, preparing custom reports and logs, modifying and coding data, and printing and organizing images. Delivers legal application and litigation database training to case teams.

What You Need to Succeed: Summation, iBlaze; Concordance, Trial Director, Access, Sanction, Access, IPRO, LiveNote, Casemap, MS Access, and other software programs. Ability to work under stress and meet critical deadlines. Knowledge of litigation process from initial filing through trial. Excellent interpersonal skills to communicate with all levels of personnel. Strong organizational skills with the ability to multi-task.

Experience in managing large electronic discovery matters from inception. Ability to work independently and as part of a cross-functional team. Flexibility to work overtime on short notice and ability to travel. Ability to solve problems by analyzing facts. Minimum of three years experience as a Project Manager or Coordinator.

General Experience/Background Required:

Paralegal litigation or related background. 5+ years experience in a litigation environment. Thorough knowledge of the litigation process. Detailed knowledge of trial procedures, discovery, document coding, scanning, court room procedures. Four-year college degree or equivalent experience preferred.

What You Need to Succeed: Major, Mid-Sized firms, in-house legal departments and government agencies and litigation support vendors.

Where You Might Find This Position: Foley & Larder; Akin Gump; DLA Piper; LeBoef, Lamb, Green & McRae; Latham & Watkins; Kilpatrick Stockton; Wilson Sonsini; Alston & Bird; Steptoe & Johnson; Clifford Chance; White & Case and many, many others.

Litigation Support Specialist, Complex Litigation

Assist paralegals and litigation support manager in management of complex litigation and large discovery matters.

Create and maintain databases for use in the management of complex litigation and large discovery matters. Assist with document review and production. Manage vendors for scanning and coding projects. Assist with electronic and document discovery. On-going support and training for litigation support applications.

E-Discovery Project Manager – Large Document Cases

Manage electronic discovery projects involving processing, organization, review and production of large document collections.

Project management, interface to clients, provide team direction/planning. Liaison to partners to use best-in-class solutions to deliver unparalleled customer satisfaction. Continuous monitoring of project progress/schedules and providing direction from changes in project requirements. Client training. Strong work ethic, excellent communications skills, track record in customer service.

Salary: $110,000 - $120,000 (New York law firms).

Project Manager – Litigation Support Projects & Vendor Management

Under the direction of the Litigation Support Manager, the Project Manager is the primary liaison to individual case teams and is responsible for promoting the effective use of litigation technologies throughout the firm or corporation.

Day-to-day tracking of litigation support projects outsourced to litigation support vendors. Work with case teams to prepare documents for processing by vendors. Ensure all assigned outsourced projects are on schedule and coordinate all vendor activity for the case teams. Coordinate requests for new databases and imagebases with the Litigation Support Analyst and assist team members in selecting and designing appropriate data structures.

Coordinate production of data and modification of database structures in consultation with the Litigation Support Analyst. This includes searching and quality control auditing of databases and imagebases, printing reports, preparing custom reports and logs, modifying and coding data, printing and organizing images.

Deliver legal application and litigation database training to case teams. Create new Concordance, IPRO, LiveNote and Sanction databases and loads data as needed. Advises team members on technical issues relating to the automation projects. Approach new needs or problems creatively and work with team members to provide effective support and solutions.

What You Need to Succeed: In-depth knowledge of electronic discovery and new amendments to the FRCP (Federal Rules of Civil Procedures). Knowledge of litigation process from initial filing through trial. Experience with Concordance, Summation, IPRO, LiveNote, Sanction, CaseSoft Suite and MS Office. Excellent interpersonal skills to communicate with all levels of personnel. Strong organizational skills with the ability to multi-task. Mandatory experience in managing large electronic discovery matters from inception. Ability to work independently and as part of a cross-functional team. Flexibility to work overtime on short notice and ability to travel. Ability to solve problems by analyzing facts and situations. Excellent organizational skills are necessary.

Salary: $80-$100,000 (Washington DC); $100-120,000 (New York).

Applied Technology Analyst - Data Mining, e-Discovery

Assist in data mining and management functions associated with the knowledge management program; process files for electronic discovery. Load and perform quality control checks on data and images Assist with project-specific user training; create training materials.

What You Need to Succeed: Bachelor's degree and 2+ years of litigation support experience working with law firms and paralegal experience. Experience with Concordance, Opticon, Summation, iConect, Trial Director, PC Docs, Microsoft Access, Microsoft Excel, ASCII data formats, Basic HTML; CD-ROM burning, macro programming and a general knowledge of applications.

Litigation Support Specialist – Technician & Analyst

This position is ideal for paralegals that are very proficient in and have a very good understanding of litigation support software (user-end). They have to be customer services oriented and people skills are a must. Very proactive and enthusiastic as this position is an outward face for the Lit Support Department.

Litigation Support Project Coordinator/Manager Online

Very hands-on Litigation Support Project Coordinator assists the Project Manager in the coordination of online reviews, drafting documents, quality control and vendor management along with the reconciling and handling of evidence and data. Extensive knowledge of software programs including Word, Outlook, Excel, Concordance, Iconect and Summation.

Litigation Support Analyst and Litigation Technician

This position is responsible for administering litigation support tools and meeting the demands of litigation attorneys and legal professionals in delivering client services. Working under the Litigation Support Manager, this position is primarily responsible for providing the Litigation Support department with scanning of documents, quality control, processing electronic discovery and assisting with the support of discovery management processing software.

IT Trainer to Attorney, Staff and Clients for Law Firm

Providing technical assistance and training to the attorney and staff on all IT related issues. Knowledge of latest software programs. Provide helpdesk support.

Legal Applications Specialist – E-Mail Applications

Run queries and technical processes with minimal supervision. Technical experience is required. Knowledge of e-mail applications such as Lotus Notes and Outlook/Exchange, and others plus MS Office on a support basis.

Litigation Support Specialist – Discovery Specialist Liaison

These requirements are typically requested for a Litigation Support Specialist: Exhibit an understanding of the litigation process, particularly discovery. Act as the liaison between litigation teams and vendors, provide guidance to legal staff. preparing for discovery, hearings, briefings, arbitrations, mediations and trial.

-Create and support document databases, indexes, transcripts, and images in CaseMap, Summation and Trial Director. Coordinate the project set up, scanning, coding, and OCRing of documents with outside vendors.

-Administer image collections and databases, including scanning documents, using OCR tools, and creating document synopses utilizing and leveraging a number of software packages.

-Assist with electronic discovery and the handling electronically stored information, working electronic discovery vendors. Assist in preparing courtroom presentation tools. Maintain preferred vendor listings

Salary range: $85- $90k base plus overtime (Los Angeles).

Paralegal Profile
Raul Estravit
Litigation Support Coordinator

Triumph & Technology
One Paralegal's Success Story

If there was ever a success story to be told about paralegals, Raul Estravit fits the profile. Soft-spoken and good-humored, Estravit has earned his stripes in the legal field. With over 20 years of experience, the 48-year old Litigation Support Coordinator can point to a diverse and remarkable career.

Starting as a paralegal in 1984, Estravit quickly discovered that technology was his ticket to success. After six years as a paralegal, he entered the litigation technology arena and never looked back. Recently recruited by the prestigious AmLaw 200 Chicago-based law firm of Winston & Strawn, Estravit works hard in the Los Angeles office coordinating litigation applications for document productions and trial presentations. He oversees the Litigation Analyst and Specialist duties, trains paralegals and lawyers on the use of litigation technology applications and works with the electronic data discovery vendors and manages EDD projects.

His climb to a top manager position in a major firm was not a straight shot. With a background working for several major law firms, he recalls a time in his career that was very different and definitely fun. "I worked on a project basis for a staffing company that sent me to work on a complex litigation case in Guam. There were a number of interesting American paralegals working on the project. Our days off in Guam were spent scuba diving and swimming. I was lucky enough to meet a paralegal also assigned to the project who became my beautiful wife", he says. "I'm obviously glad I accepted the job to go out of the country".

Estravit eventually started his own business as a trial consultant in Los Angeles. After 18 months, he was recruited by his present firm. His biggest challenge? "People who "think" they know the technology but really don't," he says. "My greatest reward, however, is using trial presentation technologies that help my clients win!"

He makes no secret he has no patience for people who make the job harder than it needs to be. However, people and technology make the job enjoyable, challenging and stimulating. "I'm in a very well paying job I love and the future is unlimited. It's a good time to be on the cutting-edge of technology".

Not one to sit home, Estravit enjoys spending his time off with his wife and children. On a clear day in Los Angeles, you'll catch him on his cabin cruiser, out in the ocean, fishing and writing music on the guitar. His best advice for paralegals: "Learn the technology, FAST," he says. It's the key to a successful future in any law firm".

Hot Tip

Sometimes you may be able to negotiate more benefits if you can't negotiate more salary.

Chapter Twenty-One
Out-of-the-Ordinary Jobs with Vendors

While we're in the process of de-mystifying some common myths, let's take a look at jobs with vendors to the legal community. Often, we get so caught up in the so-called prestige and status of the law firm; we fail to acknowledge the significance legal vendors bring to the community.

Representatives of legal vendors are often law firm career changers. We don't mean those members of law firms who "didn't quite cut it". We are talking about very good lawyers and paralegals that have chosen another avenue to leverage their legal knowledge, education and background.

Members of the legal vendor community are often well-paid and highly sought-after. Their expertise can range from trial support; litigation support; e-discovery matters; computer forensics; medical and/or nursing backgrounds; compliance; software programming; research and development and yes, even sales.

Sales positions are part the highest paying positions in the legal field. Successful sales positions are generally commission based. Some positions do pay a reasonable base salary. Top sales people have been known to earn anywhere from the low to the high six-figures. The *very* top are found in high-volume litigation support sales positions and can make anywhere from $100,000 to $300,000 per year depending upon several factors such as size of sale, complexity, number of documents involved, sophistication of software and more.

Here are just a few positions with legal vendors from very entry-level positions to higher-paying support and management positions:

Examples of Positions with Vendors & Legal Services Providers

Document Coder – Independent Contractor
Work From Home

Code documents for a litigation document coding company that creates searchable databases used to organize documents in preparation for discovery and trial.

Review documents and establish relevant fields in preparation to deliver projects to clients.

What You Need to Succeed: Well-versed in document filing and/or organization, possess an eye for detail, strong logic and comprehension skills, and have at least one year experience in the legal or litigation fields. Prior experience with a law firm, litigation support or imaging company; and/or paralegal training; or prior work experience in litigation.

Salary: Generally $10.00 - $15.00 per hour.

National Marketing Director – Litigation Support

Develop and maintain communication with new and current clients and/or partners in order to facilitate future product sales. May assist in evaluation of companies or products for marketing agreements, acquisitions, or co-promotion.

Meet or exceed sales goals for acquiring new clients and attaining other sales-related goals, as defined by senior management. Call on key contacts at target companies to assess their need for services. Conduct required number of new client appointments and calls, as determined by senior management. Effectively network employees to prospective clients. Timely documentation of business development activity to include prospective clients, key contacts and to track sales-related information and to share it as needed

What You Need to Succeed: Proven closer; track record of building and directing successful sales teams; thoroughly familiar with all aspects of litigation support services; significant exposure to litigation process; self-motivated with the ability to work independently with minimal supervision; outstanding oral and written communication skills.

Generally, a four-year degree required. A minimum of two years' experience working in a marketing and/or business development role in the legal industry is mandatory. Law degree or paralegal background is a plus.

Where You Might Find This Position: e-Discovery vendors; litigation support companies; litigation support software companies; Onsite; Merrill Corp.; Corporation Service Company; Kroll Ontrack; Smith & Carson.

Legal Consultant for Electronic Discovery Vendor

Assist attorneys, businesses, and investigators with the collection, organization, and preparation of data for review and analysis in legal matter, regulatory filings, and investigations for technology software and services company serving Data Recovery and Legal Technology markets worldwide including Electronic Discovery and Computer Forensics.

Initiate sales/marketing efforts to drive new revenues and build a brand around the company's discovery services. Responsible for direct sales/marketing efforts that develop and maintain relationships with specified law firms and in-house legal departments. Marketing includes public speaking at workshops, educational courses (CLE), seminars, and on-site law firm presentations. Legal Consultants can assist with the authoring and publication of books and articles related to the company's electronic discovery services.

Additional responsibilities can include maintaining consistent contact with strategic members of law firms responsible for the decision to outsource the electronic and paper discovery work. Ensure that the company is meeting customer expectations before and during project engagements.

What You Need to Succeed: 5+ years experience, generally from a major or Mid-Sized prestigious law firm. Knowledge of a multitude of e-discovery, litigation support, Microsoft Office and other software. A B.A./B.S. degree; paralegal certificate or J.D. degree. Plenty of trial experience. Background working with complex litigation projects.

Project Manager
Litigation Support Vendor – Model #1

Support top tier law firms and corporations. Oversee, coordinate and track progress and workflow from inception to trial. Serve as a liaison between the company and clients. Guide the team to create and deliver the right solutions by working with clients to understand their needs.

What You Need to Succeed: Experience in a litigation environment with thorough knowledge of the litigation process and an understanding of the use of technology to support litigation efforts. Knowledge of Concordance, Summation and other litigation support software, repositories and knowledge of electronic data processing for discovery. Job requires extensive overtime and plenty of travel.

Where You Might Find This Position: Litigation Support vendors; e-discovery vendors; computer forensics companies; Kroll Ontrack; Access Management; Attenex; Merrill Corp.; Aptara; EDD; Rimkus; and many more.

Project Manager
Litigation Support Vendor Model #2

The PM partners with Account Managers to provide digital solutions. The Project Manager's primary responsibility is to manage e-discovery, imaging and coding projects from project intake through delivery. Provide customer and/or technical support to paralegals, technical staff, attorneys, and vendors to coordinate production, manage and resolve issues. Companies generally offer document coding, electronic discovery and other related litigation support services.

Coordinate Coding, Electronic Discovery and other conversion projects. Responsible for entire project lifecycle including project design, documentation, status reporting, quality control and delivery. Job may require travel, extensive overtime, critical deadlines, high pressure and frequent weekend work.

What You Need to Succeed:

- Litigation support experience.
- Understanding and experience with Document Coding and EED; IPRO and Concordance.
- Familiarity with lit support applications (e.g., Summation, Opticon, various ASPs) and data manipulation tools (e.g., Access, text editors).
- Understanding of law firm environment and case life cycles.
- Excellent written and oral skills.
- Experience in digital document production.
- Advanced to expert level computer experience.
- Ability to work under pressure with tight deadlines.
- Thorough understanding of the litigation process, especially Electronic Data Discovery.
- Experience with IPRO or other litigation-specific production software.
- IT experience including network resource and backup management.

Salary: To $120,000 (in New York City).

Recruiter for Legal Staffing Companies & Temporary Agencies

Interview, recruit, place candidates in full-time or temporary positions within law firms, corporate legal departments and government agencies.

You can work the full-time placement end or the temporary placement end of the business or both for legal staffing companies. Find, interview, recruit, place, and check references, visit work sites, work with lawyers, paralegals, HR directors, Paralegal Managers, IT directors, Litigation Support Managers. Some positions are strictly recruiting; other involve recruiting and sales.

What You Need to Succeed: Background as a paralegal so you can walk the walk; talk the talk and all the rest of it. Familiarity with local legal market, law firms, potential candidates. Strong sales ability necessary.

Salaries: Generally, a base salary or a draw plus a commission. Some staffing companies pay a base salary plus a bonus based upon how well the office has done. Recruiters have been known to earn as high as $200,000 a year while others barely earn their draw.

Where You Might Find This Position: Independent staffing companies that are regional; national staffing companies such as Special Counsel; Update Staffing; Hire Counsel; Robert Half Legal; Hudson; Davidson Staffing and more.

Site Manager – Outsourced Document Management Services

Manage day-to-day operations of a 24/7 copy/print site within a major law firm as an outsourced document management services company.

Train and develop staff; provide great customer service. Develop and implement action plans to meet client expectations. Compile data for the training for management reports, profit & loss statements, purchase orders, staffing, client reports, and more.

What You Need to Succeed: At least 5 years of hands-on managerial experience in the legal world, and an orientation for customer service. Able to manage the litigation process from intake to completion, QC every step of the way, and communicate with the high end management at the firm. Bring new ideas and continuous improvement to the department. Prior litigation support experience is a must. Intermediate experience with the Microsoft Suite, IPRO, DOCS, Summation and Concordance. Ability to manage a team with a proven track record. Team building skills are also an integral part of this job, so being able to take ownership of projects and team members is essential.

Trial Technician for Trial Presentation & Graphics Vendor

Trial technicians work with attorneys and paralegals in setting up trial presentation software for and during trial. Provide Electronic Multi-media Trial Presentation for law firms, government agencies and corporate legal departments.

What You Need to Succeed: You must be proficient with trial presentation software and have knowledge of litigation database software. Experience presenting evidence electronically in a courtroom and working closely with the litigation team. Ability to travel.

Where You Might Find This Position: Legalink; Access Management; trial presentation vendors; videographers; jury consultants; graphic presentation companies.

Manager, Digital Conversion Solutions

Works with sales and operations team members to develop customer specific proposals. This is a hands-on management position and serves as the liaison between the vendor and customers to provide support for implementing process and technology-based solutions.

Serve as liaison between vendor and client and with strategic alliance partners (coding, electronic evidence, etc.). Responsible for the design, set up, tracking, management, delivery, and quality of scanning, coding, printing, e-discovery, and trial services projects. Manage the document imaging staff. Prepare project status reports. Prepare and maintain cost analysis reports for projects. Coordinate client billings for projects. Support sales efforts through client meetings, proposal generation, project qualification, and training focused on PBMS offerings. Responsible for understanding project requirements, production procedures and meeting established production goals with acceptable quality levels.

What You Need to Succeed: B.A./B.S. degree plus experience in litigation support/imaging from a large law firm or imaging center. Working knowledge of IPRO suite of imaging production tools, Microsoft Access and Windows 2000 through XP, Adobe, and familiarity with Summation, Concordance, Litigator's Notebook, Introspect, DB TextWorks, Alchemy, and more.

Experience with large-scale document production and trial preparation. Experience as a supervisor for the control and management of production processing tasks including document prep, scanning, scan QC, coding, code QC, print reassembly, print QC, PDF naming/QC, data verification or other production-related tasks.

Proficiency with scanning hardware/software and poor image exception handling. Proficiency in data capture and entry of information extracted from legal documents used in litigations and merger & acquisition projects. Proficiency in all hardware and software utilized including copiers, printers, and multi-function devices. The ability to manage multiple projects and deadlines and to allocate resources accordingly.

Presentation skills required to support sales team on client calls. Ability to train employees. Work flexible hours, including holidays, along with the necessary overtime to meet the demands of the center's clientele. Some travel required.

Where You Might Find This Position: Litigation support vendors; scanning and coding companies.

Regional Sales Manager - Facilities Management Vendor

New account development for organization providing management of copy, mail, imaging, supply, records, reception, desktop publishing, shipping and receiving and other administrative services for law firms and other large corporations. Charged with increasing company revenues and managing sales and operations in the region. Primary function is new business development.

What You Need to Succeed: Passion for legal industry; management experience; lots of legal field contacts.

Salary: Base pay plus commission. Pay is based on gross profit margin. Commissions are paid for the lifetime of the contract.

Legal Process Outsourcing in India – Senior Level Position

There is a controversial current trend for some paralegal jobs to be outsourced to India. Here is a senior level opportunity with a legal process outsourcing firm in India. This is a new set up in India and the company is engaged in litigation work for North American clients. They are looking for 'Litigation Expert – US' who would be among the top most authorities in India and responsible for setting up the entire operation. Manage litigation functions and provide supervision, training and quality control. The position is challenging in terms of roles and responsibilities. The desired profile would be a US trained law professional with 10 years experience. This position is based in Chennai, India.

Hot Tip:

If you are seeking a
position in a corporation and
your goal is to advance within
the company as far as possible,
be sure you ask "How many
vice-presidents have come
up through the legal
department?"

If the answer is
none, you may
want to reconsider
the position.

Jeannie Johnston

Founder, ParalegalGateway.com
Account Manager, Brown & Gallo LLC
Atlanta, GA

Leaving the Field Is Not An Option

Jeannie Johnston, paralegal, entrepreneur and legal vendor talks.....
I am originally from Warner Robins, Georgia and graduated from Athens
Technical College in 1991 with an AS Degree (ABA Approved Program) in
Paralegal Studies. I moved to Knoxville, TN where I lived for four years.
Then, I moved to Atlanta where I live now.

After school, I found it was difficult to obtain a position as a Paralegal
secondary to lack of on-the-job experience. I took a job in a law firm as a
courier and was promoted to Legal Secretary and eventually Paralegal. At the
time, I hated having to take a position that was not what I had studied however,
looking back, the experience was invaluable and I wouldn't trade it for anything.

**You have a couple of positions you hold at once. What is your current
position?**
In addition to being the Founder/President of Paralegal Gateway, Inc.

(ParalegalGateway.com), I recently was asked to join Brown & Gallo, LLC as a strategic Account Manager to promote their court reporting services to Paralegal and Legal Assistant communities.

What was your thought process for coming up with the idea for ParalegalGateway.com?
In 2001 I was surfing the net looking for other Paralegals to connect with and became frustrated when I realized there really wasn't a place to meet others in the profession. I had a hobby of web design so, I decided to create a place myself and ParalegalGateway.com was born. We now have the largest Yahoo! Group on the internet for Paralegals and the main site has expanded to include a weblawg, career center, online seminars, paralegal-focused articles and much more!

You're now working for a vendor after a lot of years in the law firm. What was it that interested you in making the change to "the other side"?
I learned about the opportunity with Brown & Gallo through a friend of mine in the recruiting industry. We both thought that with my connections within the legal community, the Account Manager position would be a great fit and so far, it has been just that.

You seem to be pretty savvy about the working world.
Well, I've been working since I was 15 years old so I've held several different jobs including a waitress, a disc jockey, and an office manager for a rental company, a hostess, a courier, a legal secretary and a Paralegal. Also, I tried my hand at legal recruiting for about a year and a half.

Would you mind if I asked your age (or decade)?
I'm thirty-eight.

What can you tell us about what you have learned over the past years?
I really had to learn how to let go of control in many instances and realize that it is okay to ask for assistance when you need it. You can't do everything on your own. You'll burn out if you do.

Setting up ParalegalGateway.com must bring great job satisfaction.
I love knowing that ParalegalGateway.com has really helped so many people. I receive e-mails from students and Paralegals who express how much it has meant to them and it really makes all the time and money that has been spent well worth it.

Are you affiliated with any associations?
Yes. The National Federation of Paralegal Associations and the Georgia Association of Paralegals.

With all of these busy days in your life, what do you do for fun?
Run/walk, surf the net, watch Court TV and sing/write music with my
husband.

Out of all of your jobs, what type of position most interests you?
A position that allows me the opportunity to make a difference in the lives of
others. If that means giving them a shoulder to cry on or making their life a bit
easier with great deposition services, it doesn't matter. As long as I know I've
helped out.

What is it that is compelling you to stay in the paralegal field?
I have a sincere loyalty to this profession. Additionally, I LOVE the law and
being around others who enjoy it too.

Do you have any thoughts about doing something else entirely?
I guess since I'm an Account Manager for a Court Reporting firm, I'm not
technically a practicing Paralegal. However, once a Paralegal, always a Paralegal
I say! All we need now is a 12 Step Program; "Hi, my name is Jeannie and, I'm
a Paralegal." "Hi, Jeannie." LOL!

What advice would you give paralegals looking to leave the law firm?
I think that there are so many great opportunities out there for someone who
has been a Paralegal. Legal Recruiting, Legal Software Account Managers, etc.
My experience has been that Paralegals tend to be very tenacious individuals
and there really isn't anything they can't do.

**Were you scared when you left the law firm behind for a brand new
adventure?**
Not really. I was excited about the idea of trying something new.

Do you have any regrets? How is it working for a vendor?
No regrets at all. It's really very cool. I get to continue to "hang out" with
Paralegals and offer them great services at the same time. Also, because of my
experience as a Paralegal, I am afforded the opportunity to let the Vendors
know what can be done better, different, etc. to meet the particular needs of
Paralegals.

**Be honest. If you had access to a genie and she granted a wish to do it
over.....**
Honestly, if I had my life to live over again, I probably would not have chosen
another vocation. I say this a lot, however I sincerely mean it ... "Paralegals
rock!"

Hot Tip

"Promote yourself and the experience you DO have. For instance, from 1978 to 1984 I was an aircraft mechanic. That was 20+ years ago but I still keep it on my resume. A career counselor told me it is irrelevant experience so I should leave it off.

Well, guess what? That "experience" has gotten me interviews for paralegal positions! One position was for product liability. The attorney felt with my mechanic aptitude, I would be better suited to speak with their experts about the working of the product!

My military experience, well, to me that says I am used to hard work. I can handle stress and I am a committed employee. My experience as a restaurant manager shows I can work with all types of personalities. I take responsibility and I'm organized.

Put YOUR spin on the experience you have to fit their needs! You'll be surprised".

Charlene Healy, Paralegal

Chapter Twenty-Two

Going Postal

The Good Side of Government Jobs

There's a misconception going around about government jobs. It's not the underpaid or overworked grind you might think it is. Once thought of as routine, repetitious and low-paying positions, government jobs were not first in mind when it came to choosing a paralegal position. Somewhere along the line, the government realized that in order to attract top quality candidates, it needed to compete with the private sector. Today, comparable starting salaries culminating in top salaries of $85,000 are no longer unheard of for paralegal positions in the government!

According to the Department of Labor, salaries in government swing widely. If the salary here seems low to you, remember that the DOL gives a national average that can bring down the figure in major metropolitan cities. Just a quick glimpse:

Federal Government	$59,370
Local government	38,260
Legal services	37,870
State government	34,910

If you have never researched government positions or haven't done so in a long time, now might be the time. From city, state, county, and federal government to state and federal agencies, paralegals has become an integral part of the system. Sophisticated duties, interesting positions and good salaries have all become part of the government's lure to attract excellent candidates.

Government jobs exist in areas you probably never thought existed. Have you ever thought about taking your skill set and working for the CIA? How about working on an Indian reservation doing tribal law? Can you see yourself assisting troubled children in family court? Perhaps you'd like to work directly for a judge or assist attorneys in the SEC with identity theft and securities fraud investigations. Or, you might want to assist the DA prosecuting criminals and assisting victims of crime. It does take someone who can be tough while in that environment. Don't be misled by what you see on TV. Actually working in the criminal field is much different than portrayed on shows.

Each city, county and state has a multitude of government positions. The Federal government has paralegal positions across the U.S., and not just in Washington, D.C. The U.S. Post Office, the FBI, the FTC are just a very few of the Federal positions available. Interestingly, the Department of Justice is the largest employer of paralegals in the entire U.S. followed closely by the Department of the Treasury. To find these positions, you need to locate the job website for each department or agency and apply separately.

According to the Dept. of Labor, the duties of paralegals who work in the public sector usually vary within each agency. In general, paralegals analyze legal material for internal use, maintain reference files, conduct research for attorneys, and collect and analyze evidence for agency hearings. They may prepare informative or explanatory material on laws, agency regulations, and agency policy for general use by the agency and the public. Paralegals employed in community legal-service projects help the poor, the aged, and others who are in need of legal assistance. They file forms, conduct research, prepare documents, and, when authorized by law, may represent clients at administrative hearings.

The paralegal position you are seeking in the government might have a different name. It could be a legal assistant, legal analyst, paralegal specialist, legal paraprofessional or other title. It's probably best to review as many job descriptions as possible to find out if your skills translate.

Don't overlook the fact that the hiring process can take a long time. The application process can involve endless forms and your resume must be written in a format conducive to government requirements. Three to six months can pass before you hear if you even have an interview. Patience can pay off, though. You can find yourself with an exciting position you never even dreamed of.

Where to Find Government Positions

It's a long list compounded with the fact that some of the interesting jobs you find might not be located in your city or state. You may contemplate relocating. Here are just a few government employers you're going to want to check out:

Federal Government Employers

The CIA

The FBI

Department of Justice

Department of the Treasury

Federal Trade Commission

Department of Labor

U.S. Attorney's Office

Securities & Exchange Commission

Internal Revenue Service

Federal Communications Commission

Federal Aviation Agency

Small Business Administration

U.S. Post Office

Office of the Attorney General

Prison Systems

Department of Information and Innovation

Social Security Administration

Department of the Interior

Department of Defense

Department of Homeland Security

Immigration & Customs Enforcement

The U.S. Coast Guard

State and County Employers

State Courts

Department of Commerce & Labor

District Attorney's Office

Dept. of Water & Power

County Attorney's Office

Public Defender's Office

Office of Attorney General

The Sheriff's Office

Department of Human Resources

Governor's Office

Legal Aid Society

City Employers

The Mayor's Office

City Attorney's Office

Dept. of Water & Power

Police Departments

School Districts

Council for Children

Federal Defender Paralegal - Boston, MA. 11 Lawyers

Representing criminal defense, this office of 11 lawyers representing indigent defendants accused of federal crimes sought an intelligent, enterprising, responsible person with excellent organizational ability and analytical skills to handle a variety of tasks related to criminal defense, including trial preparation and sentencing. Works with clients recovering from substance abuse in a court-sponsored program. Experience and/or training working in rehabilitative programs or with individuals in recovery useful.

New York City Mayor's Office of Labor Relations and Government / Public Law, Litigation, Public Hearings

Join a hearings unit within a government department based in New York, U.S.A. Assist the director of unit in conducting formal hearings and conferences. A candidate with certificate from an accredited paralegal program and/or a B.A. degree from an accredited college will be preferred. Must have excellent writing and oral communication skills.

Salary: $25K-$34K (NYC).

Contracts Paralegal for County Attorney's Office

Prepare various types of contracts, assisting with regulatory filings, maintaining a database, analyzing statutes and regulations and conducting legal research on the Internet. A Four-year degree and/or paralegal certificate preferred.

Litigation/Criminal Law Paralegal for The Central Intelligence Agency – (CIA) – General Paralegal Support

Paralegal (GS-9 to GS-11): Provide case management, legal research, case-cite verification, blue book citations and general paralegal support to the office of General Counsel. Support legal issues relating to foreign intelligence, counter-intelligence activities and civil and criminal litigation. Track financing for terrorists.

What You Need to Succeed: Paralegal certificate and a broad range of experience in the legal profession. Ability to research, analyze and organize effectively. Internet (LEXIS-NEXIS and PACER) and legal research skills required. PC skills; and strong written and oral communications skills. Two years experience required.

Salary: $44,865 - $70,558 (in Washington, D.C.).

Human Resources Analyst/Employment Paralegal-County Sheriff – Family/Medical Point of Contact

Function as a family/medical specialist point of contact for supervisors and employees related to family/medical policies and processes. Develop family/medical leave forms, program refinements, and training manual. Assist with performance management and career development issues and diversity related initiatives. Function as a resource to commands/employees on problems/issues and assists in day-to-day EAP activities.

Bachelor's degree in human resources management, public administration, business administration or related field and 2+ years' professional experience in human resources administration. Demonstrated proficiency in computer skills including, Microsoft Office Outlook, Word, Access, and Excel. Prior work as a Paralegal a plus.

Research and Government Paralegal for Law Firm

Research law, investigate facts, and prepare documents. Prepare export and import licenses and other submissions to governmental agencies including the departments of State, Defense, Commerce, the FAA, and state and local governments.

Draft responses to government's requests; prepare international and defense trade matters documents, aviation certifications, and contracts for review approval; prepare closing binders; draft and file articles of incorporation, by-laws, and corporate minutes; conduct legal research and prepare memoranda of law.

What You Need to Succeed: 4-6 years' experience as a corporate paralegal. Extensive software proficiency in database, word processing, time-keeping, practice management, spreadsheet, and presentation applications.

Salary: $55,000.

Litigation Paralegal for National Association of Securities Dealers (NASD) – Investigative and Legal Support

Provide investigative and legal support to the enforcement centers. Perform legal research. Prepare for on-the-record respondent testimony and off-the-record customer interviews.

Assist with investigative tasks. Review and synopsize transcripts. Assist with preparing for hearings. Analyze and prepare exhibits. Cite-check and brief pleadings. Prepare tables of contents and tables of authorities. Review disciplinary affairs documents.

What You Need to Succeed: Bachelor's degree and/or paralegal certificate or significant relevant experience. Experience in a legal setting preferred.

Proficiency in Lexis/Nexis. Proficiency in Excel, Access, iManage, Summation.

Real Estate Financing Paralegal - Housing Department
City of San Jose, California Housing Department

Preparation and/or review of real estate loan documents, closing of escrows for real estate financing transactions (including review of preliminary title reports and title policies). Experience as a real estate paralegal in closing of escrows and complex real estate financing transactions for residential development.

What You Need to Succeed: B.A. degree; 3 years of increasingly responsible paralegal work experience and 1 year of which must be at a level equivalent to an Associate Legal Analyst with the City of San Jose

Salary: $60,923.20 - $74,068.80 (San Jose, CA).

Paralegal Supervisor – County of San Diego, CA

Provide first-line supervision subordinate paralegals. Provide technical guidance; interview, train and evaluate paralegal performance. Identify and resolve division/unit procedural problems; provide input into budget matters, service and supply requisitions, and plan divisional work flow and activities.

Bankruptcy/Corporate/Insurance/Litigation/Real Estate/Criminal Law Paralegal
City Attorney of Tualatin, OR

We've hardly ever run across such a varied position: Compile and codify ordinances. Prepare and coordinate updates to the municipal and development codes. Maintain and update online versions of codes utilizing various software programs. Prepare written legal analysis from statutes, recorded judicial decisions, legal articles, treaties, constitutions, and legal codes for City Attorney. Draft reports, summaries, ordinances, and motions.

Prepare briefs, pleadings, appeals, contracts, buy-sell agreements, closing papers and binders, and deeds. Investigate factual claims. Schedule witness testimony. Provide written analysis and recommendations on proposed legislation. Investigate facts and law to determine causes of action. Prepare affidavits and subpoenas. Track and coordinate bankruptcy cases. Assist in discovery requests and coordinate discovery.

Maintain fiscal records and preparation of budget. Assemble records for land use board of appeals cases. Knowledge of city regulations and procedures in answering public inquiries. Act as municipal court clerk. Track citations. Answer questions from the public. Prepare for and attend court. Arrange and track tow appeals, set hearings. Receive limited direction from the municipal court judge.

Legal Research Assistant – Alabama State Personnel Department

Conduct research into legal problems arising in connection with the operation of state departments and agencies, in the preparation and interpretation of basic legal documents, and in the handling of routine administrative duties. Assist staff attorneys by performing routine research into legal sources.

What You Need to Succeed: Graduation from an accredited legal assistant or paralegal program; legal assistant or paralegal certificate as well as 1+ year of experience in legal research work.

Salary: $26,620.80-$46,788.00 (Alabama).

Nurse/Paralegal
Office of the Attorney General, Arizona

Prepare and present the defense of the medical malpractice lawsuits and medical aspects in other civil rights and tort litigation in the civil division, liability management section. Under supervision of the medical malpractice attorney, perform record reviews, organize files, perform medical research, interview witnesses, coordinate with experts, draft discovery, respond to discovery, prepare trial memos on medical issues, prepare witnesses to testify, prepare medical-legal exhibits, and assist at trial.

What You Need to Succeed: Graduate from an accredited school of nursing with 3+ years of experience in health care delivery systems that included treatment program planning and medical services assessments.

Salary: $33,983 - $55,305 (Maricopa County, AZ).

Litigation and Criminal Law Paralegal – County Attorney Case Preparation for Travis County Department

Provide legal assistance in the case preparation of the criminal cases of mentally ill or mentally retarded misdemeanor defendants. Provide legal research support. Review, analyze and organize case-related material required for court presentation and criminal courts. Draft pleadings, discovery, motions, affidavits, and subpoenas. Coordinate the work of secretarial support staff.

What You Need to Succeed: Equivalent to a Bachelor's degree in public or business administration or directly related field. Paralegal certificate from a professionally recognized paralegal/legal assistant program. 2+years experience.

Litigation Paralegal, Legal Aid, Housing Law, Section 8

Screen clients in the areas of housing law, Section 8 and other housing subsidy programs and housing-related public benefits. Advocate on behalf of clients, both orally and in writing, with workers at various agencies to secure government benefits and subsidies and charitable rent arrears grants, as well as with landlords (and their attorneys). Help clients complete applications for assistance in paying rent filling out and filing pro se court documents. Attend negotiation sessions, court proceedings and act as a liaison to court personnel.

Litigation Paralegal Chicago Dept. of Human Resources

Assist attorneys in all phases of pre-trial, trial and post-trial functions from routine to complex nature; collect and organize documents to respond to subpoenas and requests; assist in motions, trials and depositions; conduct legal research; research and analyze statutes, judicial decisions and legal codes; prepare and summarize summonses, motions and subpoenas; abstract depositions, briefings and complex transcripts; prepare answers and discovery; motions, pleadings and claims; interview witnesses; index and files court documents and depositions; prepare exhibits; appear in state or federal court to file documents on behalf of the city.

What You Need to Succeed: Bachelor's degree and a paralegal certificate from an ABA-approved paralegal training program.

Salary: $41,496.

Antitrust and Trade Regulation, for the Federal Trade Commission

Legal Assistant (OA)-DEU, GS-0986-05/06 Assist the Merger III Division attorneys in investigations, litigation, and in division activities. Provide administrative, document management, secretarial, and clerical support. Provide legal assistance and case support.

Assist in preparation of pleadings, assembly of exhibits, and preparation of exhibit lists for federal district court filings and other litigation matters. proofread and cite check memoranda, briefs; perform limited legal research; Perform factual research tasks such as organizing filing systems for court cases, managing court docket tickler systems, and obtaining information at state and local agencies. Respond to inquiries from consumers, businesses, and government agencies.

Salary: $30,386-$44,032 (Washington, D.C.).

Employment Litigation Paralegal, Idaho Commerce & Labor

Assist 3 partners and 2 associates. Handle medical records procurement and analysis to assist in defense-oriented workers' compensation and litigation. The candidate should have 3-5 years of experience as a paralegal (certificate preferred).

Administrative Legal Assistant - Council for Children

Join a non- profit organization based in Charlotte, U.S.A. Provide legal representation for children.

Litigation Paralegal - Department of The Interior

GS-950-7 (DEU) Review cases received on appeal for completeness; Search for and summarize relevant statutory and/or regulatory laws for use of attorneys and judges in preparation of decisions. Prepare summaries of facts in cases and legal arguments raised by parties in appeals, incorporating legal references and points of law. Compose orders related to pending appeals. Compilation of reports required by the Chief Judge, Interior Board of Land Appeals, or the Director, Office of Hearings and Appeals. Review Board of Land Appeals decisions and opinions to ensure that final decisions and orders conform. Finalizes Board decisions and orders in proper format using the full range of features available through word processing software. Prepare final IBLA decisions for posting to the OHA website.

Education: one full year of graduate-level education or a four-year degree demonstrating Superior Academic Achievement or one full year of specialized experience equivalent to the GS-05 level or combination of education and experience.

Salary: $37,640 - $48,933.

Public Defender's Office – Indigent Defense Services

Work with clients, clients' families, and the general public assisting with the delivery of indigent defense services by the Public Defender's Office in Dalton, GA. Conduct legal research, investigate facts, and prepare legal documents. Assist the public defenders in preparing for trials and hearings. Draft pleadings, discovery documents, motions, briefs.

What You Need to Succeed: Some college-level courses or graduation from an accredited 2 year college or university with a certificate in Paralegal Studies or a related field and 3+ years of professional related experience including 1+ year of experience working in a clerical or administrative role. A paralegal certificate is a plus. Spanish language skills are essential.

Health Care Paralegal Specialist – State of Florida

Draft and prepare orders, motions, notices, final judgments, final orders, recommended orders, and stipulation agreements to be filed in circuit, county, appellate, and federal courts and administrative proceedings. Prepare case summaries, pleadings, orders, and summons. Maintain case files, court calendars, and litigation timetables.

Work closely with clerk of the court, judicial assistants, private attorneys, court reporters, and staff. Research specific rules and laws. Interview witnesses. Perform legal research, gather factual information and conduct interviews. Assist during trials. Answer questions involving interpretation of policies and procedures and standard legal questions previously researched by the attorney.

In the event of a disaster, report for duty during and/or after the disaster as directed.

What You Need to Succeed: High School Diploma. Working knowledge of departmental structure, agency policies, and related legal activities. Knowledge of laws, legal codes, court procedures, precedents, government regulations, executive orders, agency rules, and, the democratic political process.

Salary: $23,645 - $28,000.

Litigation Paralegal - U.S. Dept. of Justice - Antitrust Division

Perform legal and factual research in antitrust cases and matters. Maintain an accounting system for all materials to be used as exhibits in grand jury proceedings and trials. Prepare and organize charts, graphs, tables of content, indexes, and tables of authorities for legal briefs, memoranda. Travel to the site of trial, grand jury, discovery, and others.

What You Need to Succeed: One year of specialized experience equivalent to at least the GS-5 grade level OR Graduate education; OR Combination of graduate education and specialized experience. OR Undergraduate degree and superior academic achievement. OR b. Earned election to a national scholastic honor society that meets the requirements of the Association of College Honor Societies other than freshman honor societies; OR c. Earned a grade point average (GPA) of 3.0 or higher on a 4.0 scale based on 4 years of undergraduate courses OR d. Earned a GPA of 3.5 or higher on a 4.0 scale based on all completed undergraduate courses in major.

Salary: $37,244 - $48,417 for Paralegal Specialist, GS-0950-07/07 (Dallas).

Litigation Paralegal Specialist; Department of Justice, (DOJ) Criminal Division; Computer Crime & Intellectual Property

Prepare memoranda summarizing allegations, facts, and results of investigations worldwide for section chief or higher level division officials on domestic and international issues. Review investigative reports; analyze facts presented, research applicable case and statutory law, regulations and department policy and prepares department position statements. Participation in witness interviews; attendance and assistance at trial; research and preparation of trial books and pleadings; and other tasks as a member of an investigative trial team.

Draft responses to Congressional and citizen correspondence on computer crime and intellectual property issues. Assist in the policy area, on legislative proposals; participates in presentations and compiling training materials; perform international and domestic travel; and assist in the management of office website. Qualifications required: Must have one year of specialized experience at a level close to the work of this job as outlined in the Office of Personnel Management Qualifications Handbook.

Salary: $37,640 - $72,421 (Paralegal Specialist, GS-0950-07/11, Washington, D.C.).

Special Victims Team - Office of the Prosecuting Attorney in Thurston County, WA

Assist the Prosecuting Attorney in child abuse cases, sexual assault and related cases. Investigation and fact-finding skills, legal research abilities necessary.

Family Support Paralegal - Family Support Division, Superior/State Court Systems

Assists the Prosecuting Attorney in Family Court to determine paternity, and to establish, modify and enforce child support orders. Aggressively pursues parents who have failed to pay child support payments.

Paralegal for the Securities and Exchange Commission

The SEC employs paralegals to work in the legal offices at the SEC headquarters in Washington, D.C. and in the regional offices in eleven cities nationwide.

Paralegal for the Federal Bureau of Investigation

The FBI hires paralegals. However, at this writing, we were unable to obtain any job descriptions. SEE Resources for job site.

Part-Time Paralegal for MTA - New York

Support the General Counsel, Deputy General Counsels and staff attorneys including legal research, drafting and preparing legal memoranda, aide in the management of cases, interpret legal department policies and State statutory provisions to others including MTA staff, its agencies, and members of the public and government officials.

- Interpret Legal Department policies and State statutory provisions to staff of MTA, agencies, the public, and government officials.

- Research and analyze complex legal issues and statutes; prepare reports and memoranda.

- Prepare legal notices of changes in rules, arrange for publication of notices of proposed changes and final adoption of changes to assure compliance with the New York State Public Authorities Law and the New York State Administrative procedure Act.

- Manage caseloads and maintain control of all relevant data and documentation.

- Prepare and review subpoenas, summonses, motions, affidavits, notices, resolutions, closing documents and other legal documentation.

- Assist attorneys in more difficult forms of legal proceedings, transactions, programs and projects, including appearances before judges.

- Perform a wide variety of tasks for attorneys including monitoring pending legislation, and assist in computerized research.

- Assist recording real estate documents.

What You Need to Succeed:

- Knowledge of: Legal Research, Corporations, Litigation, Real Estate and Mortgages, Criminal Law and Canons of Paraprofessional Responsibility.

- Knowledge of New York State Freedom of Information Law and State Administrative Procedure Act helpful.

- Knowledge of WestLaw and Lexis.

- Successful completion of a course in general legal assistant practice from a school approved by the American Bar Association.

Salary: $23.00 - $31.00 per hour.

Additional Government Positions to Consider

Office of the Attorney General – Consumer Protection

State Attorney General's Office – Water Rights

Paralegals in Drug Court

U.S. Post Office

Hot Tip

Don't negotiate salary by telling a prospective employer how much you need. Negotiate from the standpoint of how much you are worth.

Betty Schmidt
Division of Administrative Law Judges
Lexington, KY

The Judge's Paralegal

When Betty Schmidt decided to change careers after working in a hospital for 15 years as a Registered Nurse, she decided to apply for a job at the University of Louisville. Twelve years later and with tons of experience as a liaison to the University Council where she was exposed to administrative law and labor relations brought her to another epiphany – go for a paralegal certificate. And, thankfully, she's never turned back.

This 56-year old dynamic personality now works as a state employee for the Commonwealth of Kentucky, Environmental and Public Protection Cabinet, Division of Administrative Law Judges. She reports to an Administrative Law Judge who decides workers' compensation cases. "I worked in several Louisville law firms getting experience in workers' compensation law as well as medical malpractice law. It was this experience that enabled me to be hired for my present position," she says. "I've been very happy in my present position for a little over eight years now."

Her primary responsibility is the writing of the judge's opinions and orders. During slack time, she may do data entry, answer questions posed by attorneys and law firm personnel, prepare the judge's docket for hearings, and file pleadings. "I love my job," says Schmidt. "I don't even feel like I'm an employee while working. Each day becomes more challenging and interesting as the weeks go by".

She loves the freedom in her job to set my own pace and organize her day as she wants to, as long as she meets deadlines. "I close my door when it gets too noisy. I love having my own office and to shut the door when I want."

The job also allows her to have a life: playing tennis with friends every morning; holding the position of president of her church class; singing in the choir and don't leave out traveling. She's currently planning a two-week visit to Poland.

What has been some of the challenges? "While working as a paralegal in a law firm, she had to prepare all documents necessary for a trial. The final deadlines were sometimes tough. Working in the wee hours of the night, making exhibits, preparing trial notebooks, and preparing power point presentations for the judge got tough. "So much work to do and not having the necessary time. Sometimes I was so tired, my fingers just wouldn't hit the correct keys on the computer keyboard. I really worked hard to meet the deadline. And, then to be told the next morning that the trial was cancelled!"

Schmidt is optimistic about the joys of the career. "I honestly find a lot of job satisfaction receiving outstanding performance awards given by difficult supervisors. It's very gratifying to know that my work is appreciated by others."

Not having to work very much overtime is another payoff in her position. "My pay is comparable to other paralegals working in private law firms," she says. "Being a state employee, I receive more benefits than those in the private industry and given more holidays."

Schmidt is all for networking. It's how she found her job. Taking an active role in the local and paralegal associations and serving several years as a board member helped her find her current position. "When looking for a change in jobs, I saw my present position listed on the association websites. I applied, took state testing and was hired."

What advice would she give other paralegals seeking to get into her specialty? "Be congenial, don't complain unnecessarily, be a member of the team, and love God. Work hard at whatever task is given and to do it to the best of your ability. You will indeed receive a blessing".

Hot Tip

If you're not sure a government position is what you want, go talk to government paralegals. Contact them through your local paralegal association. Take them to lunch or ask if you can drop by or talk on the phone for 15 minutes.

Come prepared with a set of questions and find out first hand, if this is the type of move you want to make. Paralegals enjoy helping other paralegals. If you don't ask, you'll never know.

Chapter Twenty-Three

The Military
Uncle Sam Needs Paralegals

If you are young, committed and desire to serve your country, you might want to consider a career as a paralegal specialist in the military. All branches of the military, Army, Navy, Marines, Air Force, Coast Guard and Reserves offer paralegal careers. You don't need prior experience as each branch has its own training program, usually lasting anywhere from 6 – 10 weeks.

Consider this career move very carefully. Once you're in, you can't just quit and walk away! Be sure to talk with military personnel both in and out of the service. You will get different points of view. Don't be fooled, however, into thinking that by being a paralegal, you will avoid a war zone. Not so! There have been many paralegals sent to war zones. Here is a peek at what some paralegals in the armed services do:

Provide legal services to soldiers concerning filing claims for damages to personal property arising from fire, mortars, IED's, lost baggage and more; running a tax center to assist soldiers in filing their taxes; drafting wills; running immigration workshops to help soldiers become citizens of the U.S. and help soldiers with legal issues back home such as divorce, child support, SCRA, and more.

The Army
Paralegal Specialist (27D)

Assist judges, Army lawyers and unit commanders with legal matters and judicial work. Provide legal and administrative support in international law, contract law, defense legal services and judicial legal services. A Legal Specialist is involved in:

- Researching court decisions and Army regulations
- Processing legal claims and appeals
- Preparing records of hearings, investigations, court-martials and courts of inquiry

Requirements

A high school degree and a typing speed of over thirty words per minute are required. Good hearing and clear speech are assets if you're required to read aloud at court proceedings.

Training

Job training for a Legal Specialist consists of 10 weeks, three days of instruction, where you'll learn:

- Legal terminology and research techniques
- How to prepare legal documents
- High-speed transcription
- Army judicial process

Helpful Skills

- Interest in the law and legal proceedings
- Ability to keep organized and accurate records
- Interest in business, mathematics, typing and speech
- Ability to listen carefully and retain information

Advanced Responsibilities

Supervise the operation of a command section or legal office. Act as technical guide to other soldiers. In-charge of maintaining the law library and all section files and records.

The Air Force
Paralegal

Specialty Summary: (Note: This is not an entry-level job). Manages and performs legal functions not prohibited by statute and the *Lawyers' Manual on Professional Conduct*. Perform paraprofessional and legal research functions under the supervision of a judge advocate in connection with civil law, military justice, and claims activities. Supervise administration of legal services and court-reporting activities.

Duties and Responsibilities:

Plan, organize and direct legal services personnel in the areas of military justice, claims, civil law, and court-reporting activities. Provide administrative and litigation support. Examine preliminary evidence for facts and jurisdiction over offense(s) and offender. Assist commanders and first sergeants with determining appropriate forum for disciplinary actions. Perform legal research and draft charges for court-martial. Prepare documentation required for courts-martial and Article 15 actions from investigation through final action. Act as a trial member, assist attorneys with appropriate investigations, conduct witness interviews, review case status, and discuss points to develop case strategy.

Settle claims filed for and against the United States Government pursuant to Air Force publications, applicable laws, and international agreements with foreign governments. Consult with claimants on matters such as death, personal injury, and property loss or damage. Conduct claims investigations and interviews witnesses. Perform legal research.

Interview clients for legal assistance. Prepare Powers of Attorney, wills, promissory notes, deeds and bills of sale. Function as notary public. Perform duties as a paralegal in Magistrate Court. In a deployed environment, perform duties in the international, operational, and fiscal law arenas to include conducting Law of Armed Conflict (LOAC) training, evaluating compliance with LOAC, and determining wartime Rules of Engagement.

Knowledge: Keyboard and microcomputer operation; preparing and processing claims; English grammar and composition; math; functional organization of a military legal office; interviewing techniques and legal procedures concerning military courts and boards; legal terminology and interpretations; research and utilization of legal publications and reference files; civil law matters; Air Force organization and administration; and office management.

Education. For entry into this specialty, completion of high school, and college level courses in English comprehension, math, and computers is desirable.

Hot Tip

If you are seeking a military career, bear in mind that
paralegals are not exempt from war-time duty.
You can be sent to a military zone. If this is not
acceptable, you might want to reconsider. Find out
before joining!

Chapter Twenty-Four

Creating Achievement Oriented Resumes

I can be an irritating "Ms. Know-It-All" about resume writing because I've written several books on the subject. Since I spent hundreds of hours researching the topic, I believed there just wasn't too much new out there that could capture anyone's attention. I discovered I was just a bit too off-base about no new techniques available. Seeking alternative ways to attract the attention of resume-weary prospective employers who review hundreds of the same old, same old, I actually spotted some new twists on traditional techniques.

Most Acceptable Format

Before we get to the new twists, it's important that you follow the accepted guidelines and standards of resume writing for the legal field. The chronological resume is probably the one that most employers are familiar. On it, work experience is listed in reverse chronological order (most recent job first). The period of time during which you were employed is listed first, followed by the name of the employer, city and state. The next line should be a brief description for each job. (Don't overstate your duties.)

No matter if you are an experienced paralegal trying to show career growth, or paralegal student who recently received a certificate, the reverse chronological resume is probably the safest way to go. Employers prefer to see what types of job duties you held at each position rather than lumping all your job descriptions together in a functional resume. A reverse chronological format gives prospective employers a much more secure feeling about your growth.

There is a difference in the reverse chronological format only if you are an entry-level paralegal vs. an experienced level professional. Here are three basic resume writing rules to follow based upon years of experience in the field:

1. **Entry-level**: If you are just entering the field, education section is first. List your paralegal certificate, then post-graduate degree, if any; then undergrad degree. Education is followed by experience, computer skills, language skills, and associations. Keep the resume to one page.

2. **Mid-level**: Generally 2-6 years experience Listed in reverse chronological order, the first section is work history. List your present position first. Education is after work history, followed by computer skills, foreign language skills, association work, teaching experience and other work-related activities. One page is best; two is ok if absolutely necessary.

3. **Senior-level**: Generally, 6+ years experience: Listed in reverse chronological order, follow the format for mid-level. After education, list any articles or books, speaking engagements, pro bono work, teaching experience. Here's the trick for senior level paralegals: If you don't want to go back more than 10-15 years, it's not completely necessary unless you are asked. There are times when you may NOT want employers to know you have 30 years of experience in the field. One page is still best but two pages are probably most likely.

Achievement Oriented Resume

As you gain substantial experience in the field, you are going to want to convey more than job duties. The most compelling resume you can write is an achievement oriented resume. Lots of paralegals will say that they didn't achieve anything, they just did their jobs. Perhaps so, but if you reframe your reference, you will find that you did achieve hundreds of things, you just need to dig for them. The idea is to convey the results of a problem in order to demonstrate your unique abilities and skills. For example:

Problem I Faced	Action I Took	Results
Organize 10,000 e-mails recovered in e-discovery	Researched, purchased e-discovery program; trained 3 other paralegals on program	Able to produce hot docs and smoking guns in a matter of minutes

While attorneys take full credit for wins or large transactions, paralegals need to take credit for specific projects. Don't worry if you did not single handedly save the day. If you write "Saved client $300,000 by installing new software system instead of hiring temps," the reader will most likely assume you had help with the project and you were probably not the person physically hooking up the work station, wires, computers and electronics.

Be sure to differentiate between skills and accomplishments. Cite-checking a brief isn't necessarily an accomplishment. It's a skill. But quickly cite-checking a 75- page case-heavy brief in two hours so it can be filed by 5 p.m. is an achievement. Don't be shy about recounting these achievements.

Being an excellent case manager isn't an accomplishment. It's a skill. But leading a project that resulted in finding key evidence in the case is an accomplishment.

Whenever possible, try to show how what you did to contribute to the firm's profit. This shows that you were thinking about the bottom line--and sometimes that's more important than what you actually achieved.

Where do you find your achievements? Employers want to be assured that you have grown over the years and you are not doing the same assignments you did when you first started out. In the paralegal field, growth is not always a vertical climb up an invisible ladder toward a management or partnership position. Rather, it is more of a horizontal or outward growth – more sophisticated assignments are given as a result of more years in the field. Go back and pinpoint areas where you:

- Achieved more with fewer resources
- Saved the firm, organization or client money
- Reduced costs
- Saved time
- Solved a long-standing problem
- Improved the staff or team productivity, morale or situation
- Achieved technological breakthroughs
- Reduced costs
- Improved bottom-line by maintaining high billable hours and zero to low write-offs.

We know that not everyone saves the firm $1 million per year or improves billable hours by 150%. Some people really do "just do their jobs." Still, you can find accomplishments that sound impressive, and for the purposes of this exercise, that's what counts. If you are a paralegal, chances are you have saved the day on more than one occasion. (Including finding the same original an attorney has lost 13 times.) But, a resume without accomplishments is not going to impress anyone. If your resume simply lists responsibilities, what have you really told an employer? Responsibilities are simply things that you were *supposed* to do and what you were hired to do. They don't tell the employer anything about what you *did* do. For example:

Instead of Saying:	Highlight Your Accomplishments:
Prepared pleadings; drafted interrogatories; worked with client; organized documents for trial; attended trial; prepared trial notebooks; set-up war room.	Lead paralegal on winning team of high-profile case for Fortune 1000 client. Supervised 3 case assistants from inception through trial. Drafted motions; answers; prepared hard-copy and online trial notebooks. Assisted in selection of cost saving vendors; Reviewed and analyzed RFP's curbing excess fees. Set-up state-of-the-art war room and multimedia exhibits in out-of-state proceedings.

By telling a more comprehensive story, you can actually demonstrate problem solving skills, initiative and skill excellence. To create high-impact stories, think back over the assignments you have completed and what you did to assist attorneys. Describe the initial situation, what you did to fix the problem and the result of your efforts. Then summarize your story into no more than two or three lines. Be sure to keep it brief. It's not necessary to go into great detail.

By filling your resume with stories of Problem-Action-Result achievements, you will do more than attract the firm's attention to your resume. The work you do in creating compelling stories for your resume is also preparation for acing your job interviews. You will provide interviewers with a source of questions and these achievements can be used as examples as you answer interview questions.

Avoid Using Trite, Over-Used, Boring Phrases

Using trite, over-used and boring phrases you found listed under "Action Words" in a resume writing book can get your resume placed on the bottom of the pile somewhere between "I'll think about it" and "hmmm.......Let me wait and see what else comes in" stacks. *Think like the environment you are in*: if you cannot support the facts, you are NOT believable. For example:

Don't say:	Instead:
Team player	Give an example of a team situation where you performed well.
Work well under pressure	Give a specific example of a pressured situation such as a closing, trial,

	deadline where you succeeded with excellent results.
Excellent organizational skills	Give an example of an assignment where you took a project from chaos to superbly organized.
Outstanding leadership skills	What project did you lead? Give an example.

Add Struggle

"Reduced client fees by 40%," is fine--but sounds as if it could've been achieved with one phone call to a vendor. Therefore, it's not really believable. It sounds weak and not nearly as strong as it could if "struggle" were added.

Whenever possible, add the agony of the process. Lawyers love agony. That's one reason they're in the business. Show the dragons slain, describe the 14,000-foot mountains you climbed without oxygen, and mention the bushels of broken glass you crawled across to complete your assignment. Don't exaggerate, but don't minimize, either. Let's reword the above accomplishment, adding struggle:

> *Received 140 billion e-mails in discovery from client with outdated computer systems. Working within strict budget guidelines and limited workforce, reduced and consolidated clients' vendors from six to two, negotiated deeply discounted fees for volume, and cut operating costs 40%, a savings of $323,000 per month in fees to the client."*

Getting Started

Almost all paralegals have work accomplishments but they're not always easy to see. You may have to ask for help from your colleagues. Do several drafts of your resume. Always have someone else review it. Typos and grammatical errors have a way of breeding overnight when you least expect it.

The difference between a good resume and a great resume is the character and strength of the accomplishments. Your resume should read $10,000 - $15,000 above your last salary level and it will if you take the time to accentuate your past achievements. Be sure to prioritize your accomplishments by putting the strongest ones first. You don't need to list every minor responsibility.

No matter how many years of experience you have, if your resume is full of hard-hitting real accomplishments, you'll shorten your job search considerably. Doors will open more easily. You'll be interviewed more often. Your interviews will go much better, and you'll be hired sooner which is, in the end, what you want. Good luck and happy writing!

Choose wisely but don't
let a choice paralyze you.
Consider taking a transitional
position as a bridge to a new
specialty or career that is
just right for you.

There's nothing wrong with
zig-zagging your way to the
top!

Chapter Twenty-Five
Resources and Job Search Tools

Associations

American Association for Law Librarians
www.aallnet.org

American Association for Legal Nurse Consultants
www.aalnc.org

American Association for Paralegal Education
www.aafpe.org

American Immigration Lawyers Association
www.aila.org

Association of Legal Administrators
www.alanet.org

International Association for Artificial Intelligence & Law
www.iaail.org

International Paralegal Management Association
www.paralegalmanagement.org

Lex Muni
Association of independent law firms of 20,000+ lawyers in 160 law firms.
www.lexmundi.com

National Association for Law Placement Directory of Legal Employers
info@nalp.org

National Association of Legal Assistants, Inc.
www.nala.org

National Federation of Paralegal Associations
www.paralegals.org

Standing Committee on Paralegals, American Bar Association
www.abanet.org/legalservices/paralegals

Career Strategy Books

The Paralegal Career Guide Third Edition by Chere B. Estrin (PrenticeHall)

Hot Jobs & Amazing Careers: Smart Moves for Paralegals (Estrin LegalEd)

Continuing Legal Education

The Paralegal SuperConference™, Paralegal SuperSeminars™, Paralegal Trial Institute™, Corporate Paralegal Institute™, Estrin LegalEd Virtual Seminars

Estrin LegalEd
11271 Ventura Blvd., Ste. 411
Studio City, CA 91604
818.506.8701 or 888.803.8807
info@EstrinLegalEd.com
www.EstrinLegalEd.com

West LegalEd
www.westlegaled.com

Directories

The Martindale Hubbell
www.martindale.com

Directory of Environmental Attorneys
National Directory of Criminal Lawyers
Law and Business Directory of Litigation Attorneys

Law and Business Directory of Intellectual Property Attorneys
Law and Business Directory of Bankruptcy Attorneys
Law and Business Directory of Sports and Entertainment Attorneys
Directory of Construction Law Firms

Employer Profiles

Vault.com
www.vault.com

Internet Job Sites:

Association of Corporate Counsel
www.acca.com

Beyond.com
www.Beyond.com

CareerBuilder.com
www.careerbuilder.com

Federal Bureau of Investigation
www.fbijobs.gov

Government Jobs
www.governmentjobs.com

Jobs.net
www.jobs.net

Lawfirmstaff.com
www.lawfirmstaff.com

Monster.com
www.monster.com

Jobs in Canada
Totallegaljobs.ca

Hot Jobs
www.hotjobs.com

FindLaw
http://careers.findlaw.com

Simply Law Jobs, Inc. (England)
www.simplylawjobs.com

Indeed.com
www.indeed.com

BostonWorks.com
www.Bostonworks.com

Craig's List
www.craigslist.com

Federal Jobs
www.usajobs.opm.gov

HispanicJobs.com
www.hispanicjobs.com

Jobs Online
www.jobsonline.com

LegalStaff
www.legalstaff.com

Law Crossing
www.lawcrossing.com

Paralegal Jobs.com
www.paralegaljobs.com

Totally Legal
www.totallylegal.com

National Federation of Paralegal Associations
http://paralegals.legalstaff.com

Online Paralegal Schools

American Institute for Paralegal Studies
www.aips.com

Kaplan Online
www.kaplan.com

University of Maryland University College
www.umuc.edu/programs

Washington Online
www.woli.com

Publications

American Lawyer magazine
www.alm.com

Inside Counsel
www.insidecounsel.com

Law Technology News (LTN)
www.lawtechnologynews.com

Legal Assistant Today
www.LegalAssistantToday.com

The Legal Intelligencer (Philadelphia)
www.law.com/pa

The Daily Journal (Los Angeles, San Francisco)
www.dailyjournal.com

Legal Times Washington, D.C.
www.law.com

San Francisco Recorder
circulation@therecorder.com

Resume Writing Books

The Successful Paralegal's Job Search Guide
By Chere B. Estrin (Thomson West)

Salary Surveys

Estrin LegalEd
www.EstrinLegalEd.com

Altman Weil
www.altmanweil.com

NALA
www.nala.org

NFPA
www.paralegals.org

IPMA
www.paralegalmanagement.org

Salary.com
www.Salary.com

Staffing Organizations

National:

Surge Staffing
www.surgestaff.com

Special Counsel
www.specialcounsel.com

Kelly Law
www.kellylaw.com

Hire Counsel
www.hirecounsel.com

Hudson Global
www.Hudson.com

Regional:

Biltmore Legal (Phoenix)
www.biltmorelegal.com

Professional Careers (Los Angeles)
www.procareersultd.com

Davidson Staffing (California)
www.davidsonstaffing.com

Juristaff (New York, Philadelphia, D.C.)
www.juristaff.com

Pat Taylor & Associates (Washington, D.C.)

www.pattaylor.com

Hot Gigs (New York)
www.hotgigs.com

Vendors

The Big Book of Legal Vendors
www.EstrinLegalEd.com

20 Major Law Firms
(Randomly selected)

Law Firm	Main Office	Number of Attorneys
Baker & McKenzie	Chicago	3,156
Jones Day	Cleveland	1,698
Reed Smith	Pittsburg	1500+
Morgan, Lewis	Philadelphia	1,300
Holland & Knight	Tampa	1,162
Foley & Lardner	Milwaukee	981
Morrison & Foerster	San Francisco	864
Gibson, Dunn	Los Angeles	800
Stinson Morrison	Kansas City, MO	335+
Barnes & Thornburg	Indianapolis	325
Kutak Rock	Omaha	311
Nelson Mullins Riley	Columbia, S.C.	285
Bryan Cave	St. Louis	250+
Luce Forward	San Diego	209
Wolf, Block,	Philadelphia	239
Holland & Hart	Denver	239
Baker Donelson	Memphis	230
Brown Rudnick Berlack	Boston	194

Hot Tip:

Don't negotiate salary by telling a prospective employer how much you need. Negotiate from the from the standpoint of how much you are worth.

About the Author

Chere B. Estrin is the author of eight career books including *The Paralegal Career Guide Third Edition (Prentice-Hall)* and *The Successful Paralegal's Job Search Guide (Thomson Delmar)*... Ms. Estrin, the CEO of the Los Angeles-based legal professional training organization, Estrin LegalEd and founder of The Paralegal SuperConferences™ holds a Ph.D. in Human Resources Development. She is a former executive with a Fortune 500 Corporation, an administrator in two major law firms and a successful entrepreneur. She has been interviewed by *Newsweek, The Los Angeles Times, The Chicago Tribune, Working Woman, Latina, Maxim, The Tennessean, Frontier, The Daily Journal, Entrepreneur, The New York Times* and other prestigious publications.

Ms. Estrin is the career advice columnist for *Legal Assistant Today*. The magazine named her "Career Guru" in 2001. She is a recipient of the Century City/Los Angeles Chamber of Commerce "Woman of Achievement Award"; an *Inc.* magazine "Entrepreneur of the Year" finalist; a *California Lawyer* magazine "LAMMIE" award winner, Los Angeles Paralegal Association Lifetime Achievement Award recipient and a co-founding member of The International Paralegal Management Association.

An energetic seminar leader, Ms. Estrin has been a featured and keynote speaker for many associations. She has appeared on radio and TV as well as led retreats and workshops in top law firms and corporations across the country.

She can be reached at info@estrinlegaled.com or www.EstrinLegalEd.com.